## Copyright Notice

CCNA Whiteboard: ICND1, ICND2, 200-125

Copyright © 2018 Shaun L. Hummel

All Rights Reserved. No part of this work may be sold, reproduced or transmitted in any form or by any means without written permission from the author.

## Disclaimer

This book was written as a study guide to Cisco CCNA certification. While every effort has been made to make this book as accurate as possible no warranty is implied. The author shall not be liable or responsible for any loss or damage arising from the information contained in this book.

## About The Author

CiscoNet Solutions is a certification training provider and recipient of Cisco spotlight awards for technical contributions. The certification training strategy is based on a step-by-step approach with study guides, lab training, exam notes and practice tests. It is all designed to prepare you for passing the CCNA certification exam.

# Contents

*Introduction* 11

**Section 1**     **Network Fundamentals** 13

           OSI Reference Model 13
           TCP/IP Reference Model 13
           Network Cabling 13
           Network Protocols 14
           Ethernet Media Standards 14
           Network Messaging 14
           IP Address Classes 15
           RFC 1918 Private Addressing 15
           Convert Decimal to Binary 16
           Convert Binary to Decimal 16
           Subnetting Class C Address 16
           Subnetting Class B Address 17
           IPv4 Wildcard Masks 18
           IPv4 Address Types 19
           Device Classes 19
           Traffic Domains 19
           Wireless Characteristics 20
           Network Broadcasts 20
           TCP vs UDP Comparison 20
           Application Ports 21
           IPv6 Address Characteristics 21
           IPv6 Addressing Rules 21
           IPv6 Address Types 22
           IPv6 Route Types and Prefixes 22
           IPv6 Addressing Options 23
           IPv6 Packet 23
           Cloud Service Models 23

**Section 2**     **LAN Switching Technologies** 24

           Switching Concepts 24
           MAC Address Table 24
           MAC Learning and Aging 24
           Frame Switching 25
           Ethernet Frame Format 28
           Access Ports (Data and Voice) 28
           Trunk Interface 29
           802.1q VLAN Tag 29
           Native VLAN 29
           VLAN Pruning 30

Dynamic Trunking Protocol 30
Normal/Extended VLANs 32
VLAN Trunking Protocol 32
EtherChannel 33
    PAgP Modes 33
    LACP Modes 33
Spanning Tree Protocol 34
    Root Bridge Selection 35
    PortFast 35
    BPDU guard 35
Cisco Discovery Protocol 35
Link Layer Discovery Protocol 36

## Section 3    Routing Technologies 37

Router Operation 37
Frame Rewrite 37
Time-to-Live (TTL) 37
Routing Table Lookup 37
ARP Operation 38
Route Selection 38
    Packet Forwarding 39
    Packet Discard 39
    Administrative Distance 39
Distance Vector vs Link State 40
OSPF Operation 41
OSPF Commands 42
OSPFv3 42
EIGRP Operation 43
EIGRP Timers 43
EIGRP Routing Tables 43
EIGRP Commands 44
EIGRP for IPv6 44
RIPv2 for IPv4 45
Route Summarization 45
Dynamic Route 46
Static Route 46
Floating Static Route 46
Default Route 46
Default-Information Originate 47
IPv6 Static Routing 47
Routing Table Components 47
Routing Source Codes 48
InterVLAN Routing 48
IPv4 Packet 49
TCP Segment 49

| Section 4 | **WAN Technologies** 50 |
|---|---|
| | TCP Handshake 50 |
| | Point-to-Point Protocol 50 |
| | WAN Access Protocols 50 |
| | DMVPN Advantages 51 |
| | Quality of Service 51 |
| | Traffic Shaping vs Policing 51 |
| | External BGP 52 |
| Section 5 | **Infrastructure Services** 53 |
| | DNS Commands 53 |
| | DHCP Features 53 |
| | Network Time Protocol 54 |
| | Network Address Translation 54 |
| |    Static NAT 54 |
| |    Dynamic Pool 55 |
| |    Port Address Translation 55 |
| | Hot Standby Router Protocol 56 |
| Section 6 | **Infrastructure Security** 57 |
| | Device Passwords 57 |
| | Port Security 58 |
| |    Sticky 58 |
| |    Static 58 |
| |    Dynamic 58 |
| |    Max MAC Addresses 58 |
| |    Violation Actions 59 |
| | Access Control Lists 59 |
| |    Standard 59 |
| |    Standard Named 59 |
| |    Extended Named 59 |
| |    Extended 59 |
| |    ACL-1 Example 60 |
| |    ACL-2 Example 60 |
| |    ACL-3 Example 61 |
| |    ACL-4 Example 61 |
| | RADIUS vs TACACS 62 |
| Section 7 | **Infrastructure Management** 63 |
| | SNMP 63 |
| | Syslog Server 63 |
| | Message Logging 64 |
| | Password Recovery 64 |
| | Selecting IOS Image 65 |

Startup Configuration 65
Config-Register 66
Command Modes 66
File Transfer Protocols 66
File System Commands 67
Network Programmability 68

## Section 8    Troubleshooting Systems 69

OSI Layer Approach 69
Host Connectivity 69
Operational vs Administrative 69
Network Interface States 69
Interface Errors 70
Duplex Setting 70
Trunking / DTP 71
EtherChannel 71
VLAN Trunking Protocol 71
Managing Switches 72
OSPFv2 72
EIGRP for IPv4 72
EIGRP for IPv6 73
RIPv2 for IPv4 73
Router-on-a Stick 73
Generic Routing Encapsulation 73
Access Control Lists 73
Dynamic Host Configuration Protocol 74
Hot Standby Router Protocol 74
Network Address Translation 74

## Section 9    CCNA SIM Labs 75

Troubleshooting Approach 75
show ip interface brief 75
show vlan 75
show interfaces trunk 75
show etherchannel summary 75
show vtp status 76
show ip route 76
show access-lists 76
show running-config 76

## Section 10    CCNA Supplemental Reference 79

IOS Command Reference 79
IOS Configuration Examples 91
CCNA Test Strategies 99

# Introduction

CCNA certification has become increasingly difficult and require proper preparation to pass the exam. **There is a high pass score of 82% and an average fail rate of 70% on first attempt**. The training strategy should include books, simulation labs, practice tests and exam day review. It is important to learn the fundamentals and summarize what was learned multiple times as exam day approaches. CCNA candidates should learn test taking skills as well to verify exam readiness and optimize time management skills. The simulation questions account for 40% of all exam points and is key to passing the exam. Learn a strategy with a step-by-step approach to resolve errors and answer questions.

CCNA whiteboard is a study tool designed for quick summary of protocol operation, concepts, features, addressing, design rules and configuration. There is a systems troubleshooting section as well with root cause analysis for most common network problems. The whiteboard makes the exam day review easier to refresh your knowledge before the exam and hit the ground running. Use it to create your own whiteboard as well with the paper provided at the test center. It is often difficult to adequately summarize key information from months of course training and books.

Target Audience

- 100-105 ICND1
- 200-105 ICND2
- CCNA 200-125

# Network Fundamentals

**Table 1** OSI Reference Model

| OSI Layer | Network Services | PDU |
|---|---|---|
| application | process-to-process communication, API services | data |
| presentation | data formatting, translation, encoding, encryption | data |
| session | logical communication between applications | data |
| transport | reliability, flow control, error recovery, host-to-host | segment |
| network | IP address, best path selection, next hop forwarding | packet |
| data link | media access control (MAC), physical addressing | frame |
| physical | electrical signaling, putting bits on physical media | bits |

**Table 2** TCP/IP Reference Model

| TCP/IP Model | OSI Layer |
|---|---|
| application layer | session layer, presentation layer and application layer |
| transport layer | transport layer |
| internet layer | network layer |
| network layer | physical layer and data link layer |

**Table 3** Network Cabling

| Cable Type | Usage Examples |
|---|---|
| straight-through | switch to router, firewall to router, host to switch |
| rollover | console port only |
| crossover | switch to switch, router to router, firewall to firewall |
| serial | router to CSU/DSU |

**Table 4** Network Protocols

| OSI Layer | Network Protocols |
|---|---|
| application layer | HTTP, Telnet, SSH, TFTP, DNS, FTP, SNMP, DHCP |
| presentation layer | SSL, TLS |
| session layer | PAP, CHAP |
| transport layer | TCP, UDP |
| network layer | IP, ICMP, EIGRP, OSPF, RIP, NAT, HSRP |
| data link layer | Ethernet, PPP, PAgP, LACP, STP, ARP, CDP |
| physical layer | Cabling, 802.3ae, 802.3z, T1, T3, SONET, DSL |

**Table 5** Ethernet Media Standards

| Ethernet Standard | Media Specification |
|---|---|
| 1000Base-LX/LH | Single-mode Fiber (SMF), 1000 Mbps, 10 km |
| 1000Base-SX | Multi-mode Fiber (MMF), 1000 Mbps, 220-550 m |
| Cat 5 | Copper, 100 Mbps, 100 m |
| Cat 5e | Copper, 1000 Mbps, 100 m |
| Cat 6 | Copper, 10 Gbps, 55 m |
| 1000Base-LX | Multi-mode Fiber (MMF), 1000 Mbps, 550 m |
| 1000Base-ZX | Single-mode Fiber (SMF), 1000 Mbps, 70 km |

**Table 6** Network Messaging

| Message | Description |
|---|---|
| unicast | packets sent from a single source to a single destination |
| multicast | packets sent from a single source to a destination group |
| broadcast | packets sent from a single source to all hosts on a VLAN |
| anycast | packets sent from a single source to nearest destination |

## Table 7  IP Address Classes

| Address Class | IP Address Range | Default Subnet Mask |
|---|---|---|
| Class A | 1.0.0.0 - 127.255.255.255 | 255.0.0.0 |
| Class B | 128.0.0.0 - 191.255.255.255 | 255.255.0.0 |
| Class C | 192.0.0.0 - 223.255.255.255 | 255.255.255.0 |
| Class D | 224.0.0.0 - 239.255.255.255 | Not Applicable |
| Class E | 240.0.0.0 - 255.255.255.255 | Not Applicable |

## Table 8  RFC 1918 Private Addressing

| IP Address Range | Subnet Mask | Network | Host |
|---|---|---|---|
| 10.0.0.0 - 10.255.255.255 | 255.0.0.0 | 8 bits (/8) | 24 bits |
| 172.16.0.0 - 172.31.255.255 | 255.240.0.0 | 12 bits (/12) | 20 bits |
| 192.168.0.0 - 192.168.255.255 | 255.255.0.0 | 16 bits (/16) | 16 bits |

## Binary Conversion

The following describes how to convert from IPv4 decimal notation to binary for subnetting and summarization.

- The binary system is based on ones (1) and zeros (0).
- There are 8 bits per octet, 4 octets per IPv4 address.
- The bit value is based on position.
- The bit set to 1 sets the value. The bit set to zero = 0
- There are 8 bits with 2 (nth power) so $2^8$ = 255
- Per octet: set all bits to 1 = 255, set all bits to 0 = 0

| 0 | 0 | 0 | 0 | 0 | 0 | 0 | 0 | = 0 |
|---|---|---|---|---|---|---|---|---|
| 1 | 1 | 1 | 1 | 1 | 1 | 1 | 1 | = 255 |
| 8 | 7 | 6 | 5 | 4 | 3 | 2 | 1 | bit position |
| 128 | 64 | 32 | 16 | 8 | 4 | 2 | 1 | bit value |

### Example: Convert Decimal to Binary

Converting IPv4 address 192.168.64.10 to equivalent binary number requires setting specific bits for each octet to (1) value. The sum of each octet must add up to the decimal value for each octet.

        192    .    168    .    64    .    10

**11**000000 . **10101**000 . **01**000000 . 0000**1**0**1**0

(128+64) | (128+32+8) | 64 position | (8+2)

### Example: Convert Binary to Decimal

00001010.01100100.00101000.10000000

Converting the following IPv4 binary number to decimal equivalent requires adding bits for each octet that are set to (1) value:

        10    .    100    .    40    .    128

0000**1**0**1**0 . 0**11**00**1**00 . 00**1**0**1**000 . **1**0000000

(8+2) | (64+32+4) | (32+8) | 128 position = **10.100.40.128**

**Table 9** Subnetting Class C Address

| Subnet Mask | CIDR | Subnet Bits | Subnets | Host Bits | *Hosts |
|---|---|---|---|---|---|
| 255.255.255.0 | /24 | none | none | 8 | 254 |
| 255.255.255.128 | /25 | 1 | 2 | 7 | 126 |
| 255.255.255.192 | /26 | 2 | 4 | 6 | 62 |
| 255.255.255.224 | /27 | 3 | 8 | 5 | 30 |
| 255.255.255.240 | /28 | 4 | 16 | 4 | 14 |
| 255.255.255.248 | /29 | 5 | 32 | 3 | 6 |
| 255.255.255.252 | /30 | 6 | 64 | 2 | 2 |
| 255.255.255.254 | /31 | 7 | 128 | 1 | 2 |
| 255.255.255.255 | /32 | - | - | - | 1 |

\* The number of hosts addresses does not include the network address and broadcast address. They are reserved for each subnet and are not assignable to host interfaces or device interfaces. For example 8 host bits = $2^8$ = 256 - 2 = 254

## Subnetting Example

                        **network**          | host

        **11111111.11111111.11111111.111** 00000

          255.       255.       255.     224

1. Class C subnetting = 4th octet subnetted
2. subnet multiple = 256 - 224 = 32 (0, 32, 64, 96, 128…)
3. network address of .32 subnet = 192.168.32.0
4. host range = first 5 bits = $2^5$ = 32 - 2 = 30 host assignments

- network address = 192.168.32.0
- host range = 192.168.32.1 - 192.168.32.30
- broadcast address = 192.168.32.31

**Table 10** Subnetting Class B Address

| Subnet Mask | CIDR | Subnet Bits | Subnets | Host Bits | *Hosts |
|---|---|---|---|---|---|
| 255.255.0.0 | /16 | none | none | 16 | 65534 |
| 255.255.128.0 | /17 | 1 | 2 | 15 | 32766 |
| 255.255.192.0 | /18 | 2 | 4 | 14 | 16382 |
| 255.255.224.0 | /19 | 3 | 8 | 13 | 8190 |
| 255.255.240.0 | /20 | 4 | 16 | 12 | 4094 |
| 255.255.248.0 | /21 | 5 | 32 | 11 | 2046 |
| 255.255.252.0 | /22 | 6 | 64 | 10 | 1022 |
| 255.255.254.0 | /23 | 7 | 128 | 9 | 510 |
| 255.255.255.0 | /24 | 8 | 256 | 8 | 254 |
| 255.255.255.128 | /25 | 9 | 512 | 7 | 126 |
| 255.255.255.192 | /26 | 10 | 1024 | 6 | 62 |
| 255.255.255.224 | /27 | 11 | 2048 | 5 | 30 |
| 255.255.255.240 | /28 | 12 | 4096 | 4 | 14 |
| 255.255.255.248 | /29 | 13 | 8192 | 3 | 6 |
| 255.255.255.252 | /30 | 14 | 16384 | 2 | 2 |
| 255.255.255.254 | /31 | 15 | 32768 | 1 | 2 |
| 255.255.255.255 | /32 | - | - | - | 1 |

**Table 11** IPv4 Wildcard Masks

| Subnet Mask | CIDR | Wildcard Mask |
|---|---|---|
| 255.0.0.0 | /8 | 0.255.255.255 |
| 255.128.0.0 | /9 | 0.127.255.255 |
| 255.192.0.0 | /10 | 0.63.255.255 |
| 255.224.0.0 | /11 | 0.31.255.255 |
| 255.240.0.0 | /12 | 0.15.255.255 |
| 255.248.0.0 | /13 | 0.7.255.255 |
| 255.252.0.0 | /14 | 0.3.255.255 |
| 255.254.0.0 | /15 | 0.1.255.255 |
| 255.255.0.0 | /16 | 0.0.255.255 |
| 255.255.128.0 | /17 | 0.0.127.255 |
| 255.255.192.0 | /18 | 0.0.63.255 |
| 255.255.224.0 | /19 | 0.0.31.255 |
| 255.255.240.0 | /20 | 0.0.15.255 |
| 255.255.248.0 | /21 | 0.0.7.255 |
| 255.255.252.0 | /22 | 0.0.3.255 |
| 255.255.254.0 | /23 | 0.0.1.255 |
| 255.255.255.0 | /24 | 0.0.0.255 |
| 255.255.255.128 | /25 | 0.0.0.127 |
| 255.255.255.192 | /26 | 0.0.0.63 |
| 255.255.255.224 | /27 | 0.0.0.31 |
| 255.255.255.240 | /28 | 0.0.0.15 |
| 255.255.255.248 | /29 | 0.0.0.7 |
| 255.255.255.252 | /30 | 0.0.0.3 |
| 255.255.255.252 | /31 | 0.0.0.1 |
| 255.255.255.255 | /32 | 0.0.0.0 |

**Table 12** IPv4 Address Types

| Type | Description |
|---|---|
| static | manually assigned to a network interface |
| dynamic | DHCP assigned from an address pool |
| secondary | manually assigned from a different subnet than primary address |
| loopback | logical interface manually assigned to a network device |
| gateway | layer 3 address used for access to routing services |

**Table 13** Device Classes

| Device Class | OSI Layer |
|---|---|
| bridge | Layer 2 |
| wireless access point | Layer 2 |
| wireless LAN controller | Layer 2 |
| switch | Layer 2 |
| router | Layer 3 |
| firewall | Layer 7 |

**Table 14** Traffic Domains

| Device Type | Description | Traffic Flow |
|---|---|---|
| bridge | collision domain | half-duplex |
| wireless AP | collision domain | half-duplex |
| *switch port | collision domain | full-duplex |
| VLAN | broadcast domain | not physical interface |
| router interface | broadcast domain | full-duplex |

\* half-duplex switch ports are not configured on Gigabit interfaces unless required for compatibility with third party equipment or older network devices.

**Table 15** Wireless Characteristics

| Access Point | Wireless LAN Controller |
|---|---|
| • bridge traffic<br>• MAC forwarding<br>• RF cell<br>• CSMA/CA<br>• switch uplink | • deploy / manage access points<br>• dynamic RF management<br>• MAC forwarding<br>• frame rewrite<br>• switch uplink |

**Table 16** Network Broadcasts

| Broadcast Type | Destination Address | Examples |
|---|---|---|
| Layer 2 | FFFF.FFFF.FFFF | MAC Learning, ARP, VLAN |
| Layer 3 | 255.255.255.255 | DHCP, subnet only |
| Multicast | Reserved IP address | routing protocols |

**Table 17** TCP vs UDP Comparison

| TCP | UDP |
|---|---|
| OSI transport layer | OSI transport layer |
| connection | connectionless |
| error recovery | error check / discard |
| slower | faster |
| guaranteed delivery | best effort |
| retransmission | no retransmission |
| HTTP, Telnet, FTP | DHCP, SNMP, TFTP |

**Table 18** Application Ports

| Application | Port |
|---|---|
| Telnet | TCP 23 |
| SMTP | TCP 25 |
| FTP | TCP 21 |
| HTTP | TCP 80 |
| SNMP | UDP 161 |
| DNS | TCP/UDP 53 |
| HTTPS | TCP 443 |
| SSH | TCP 22 |
| TFTP | UDP 69 |

## IPv6 Address Characteristics

- 128 bits length address
- 8 groups with 4 bits per group
- prefix (64 bit) and interface identifier (64 bit)
- multicast, anycast and unicast messages only
- Regional Internet Registry (RIR) allocated
- loopback (**::1**) and link-local address mandatory per interface
- multiple address per interface supported

## IPv6 Addressing Rules

- IPv6 is based on hexadecimal with values only from **0 to F** permitted.
- The double colon **::** is only permitted once per IPv6 address.
- Minimize multiple **consecutive** zero groups to a double colon **::**
- Delete leading zeros from a single group (**00**9F = :9F:)
- Minimize a **single** group with all zeros to single zero **:0:**
- Any IPv6 address with less than 8 groups must have a double colon that represents a single or multiple zero groups

**Table 19** IPv6 Address Types

| IPv6 Address | Description |
|---|---|
| global unicast | internet routable with global routing prefix |
| multicast | prefix FF00::/8 (send to group members) |
| unique local | private globally unique, not internet routable, starts with FD |
| link-local | auto-configured, mandatory, local subnet only, used for routing adjacency, prefix FE80::/64 |
| modified eui-64 | IPv6 host interface identifier, derived from MAC address |
| anycast | send to any member of a group that is nearest and available |
| loopback | mandatory address per interface ::1/128 |

**Table 20** IPv6 Route Types and Prefix Examples

| Route | Example |
|---|---|
| network prefix | /64 |
| default route | ipv6 route ::/0 2001:DB8:3C4D:2::1 |
| point-to-point address | /126 |
| floating static route | ipv6 route 2001:DB8::/32 serial 1/0 200 |
| static route | ipv6 route 2001:DB8:3C4D::/64 serial 1/0 FE80::2 |
| host route | /128 |
| directly connected static route | ipv6 route 2001:DB8::/32 serial 1/0 |

**Table 21** IPv6 Addressing Options

The following methods are available for assigning IPv6 addresses to interfaces.

| Method | Description |
|---|---|
| Manual | traditional method of statically assigning or configuring an IPv6 address. |
| Stateful DHCPv6 | most similar to DHCPv4 server for address assignment. |
| Stateless DHCPv6 | SLAAC is used with this method to assign only an IPv6 address and default gateway to client interface. DHCPv6 server is required for additional settings such as DNS server address for example. |
| SLAAC | Stateless Autoconfiguration (SLAAC) generates a unique link-local address based on EUI-64 format. The IPv6 address is based on the network prefix (local subnet) for each client. |

## IPv6 Packet

| Version 4-bits | Traffic Class 8 bits | Flow Label 20 bits | |
|---|---|---|---|
| Payload Length 16 bits | | Next Header 8 bits | Hop Limit 8 bits |
| 128-bit Source IP Address | | | |
| 128-bit Destination IP Address | | | |
| Payload (Data) | | | |

IPv6 Header = 320 bytes

### Cloud Service Models

- IaaS provides virtual data center services and tenant customization
- SaaS is public and provides ready web-based applications
- PaaS enables a software development environment
- Cloud enable security controls, tenant segmentation and virtualization

# LAN Switching Technologies

## Switching Concepts

The following is a list of network services provided by switches:

- switches forward data link layer traffic
- switches create and maintain the MAC address table
- switches create collision domain per Gigabit port
- switches create broadcast domain per VLAN

## MAC Address Table

Every network device and host is assigned a unique hardware address from the manufacturer called a MAC address. The purpose of a MAC address is to provide a unique Layer 2 identifier. That enables communication between devices of the same network segment (VLAN) or different segments. The switch forwarding decisions are based on the MAC address and assigned port.

- enable packet forwarding between hosts on the same VLAN
- globally unique network device identifier associated with a VLAN

The MAC (physical) address is 48 bits of hexidecimal numbering. The first 24 bits is a manufacturer OUI and the last 24 bits (bold) is a unique serial number (SN).

**OUI | SN**
**0000.00 0a.aaaa**

The switch builds a MAC address table comprised of MAC address, switch port and VLAN membership for each connected host. The switch creates a separate MAC address table for each configured VLAN. Any unicast flooding of a frame to learn a MAC address is for the assigned VLAN only.

## MAC Learning and Aging

MAC address learning occurs when a switch is started, rebooted or the aging timer expires. It is how switches learn the source MAC address of each host and create an entry in the MAC address table. MAC learning is triggered periodically when the aging time expires for an entry. The switch removes (flushes) MAC address table entries every five minutes (300 seconds) as a default. Configure the aging timer to 0 seconds to prevent entries from being flushed and MAC learning.

MAC learning is triggered per host or network device when it starts initially sending frames for communication. The switch creates a Layer 2 broadcast frame that is forwarded to all devices on a single broadcast (VLAN) domain.

The broadcast packet includes **FFFF.FFFF.FFFF** as the destination MAC address and forwards it out all ports except where the frame was learned. The port where the frame was learned is the sending host. Broadcast frames are created and never learned from an inbound switch port. The following summarizes what happens when a host sends a packet to a server on the same VLAN for the **first** time.

1. The switch adds the source MAC address of the incoming frame if it is not listed in the MAC address table.

2. The switch does a MAC address table lookup for the destination MAC address (server).

3. The switch floods the broadcast frame using destination MAC address **FFFF.FFFF.FFFF** out all ports except the port where the source MAC address was learned. It is called a **unicast flood** of a broadcast frame.

4. The server with the assigned MAC address responds with a frame that lists the MAC address for that server.

5. The switch updates the MAC address table with the MAC address of the server. That is the destination MAC address written to all frames sent from the host for any session with that server.

6. The switch forwards the frames from the host to the server based on the switch port assigned to the server.

The switch will first flood the local VLAN segment (unicast MAC flooding) to determine if the host is local. The ARP broadcast is only sent for packet forwarding between local and remote hosts on different VLANs or subnets. Unknown unicast frames are retransmitted only to ports that belong to the same VLAN

## Frame Switching

The packets sent from hosts have an IP header encapsulated in an Ethernet frame. The source and destination IP address is written to each header and required for end-to-end network connectivity. Layer 2 switches do not examine or understand IP addressing. Switches and wireless access points make forwarding decisions based on the destination MAC address in the frame. They do not rewrite MAC addressing in the frame. They only examine the source MAC address and destination MAC address. The frame header is examined for the destination MAC address. The switch does a MAC address table lookup to make a forwarding decision. The frame is then forwarded out the switch port associated with the destination MAC address. Any destination MAC address that is not local is forwarded to the router. The IP addressing does not change between source and destination.

- switches use the destination MAC address to make forwarding decisions
- switches forward frames and do not rewrite source or destination MAC address

## Frame Switching Examples

### Example 1:

Refer to the drawing where Host-1 has sent a packet to Server-1. The destination MAC address is unknown. The switch will unicast flood (learning) the frame out all ports except the port where the frame was learned from (Gi1/1). Server-1 with the matching destination MAC address receives the frame and sends a frame to Switch-1. The switch updates the MAC address table with the MAC address and associated port (Gi1/3) of Server-1.

**Figure 1** Frame Switching Topology 1

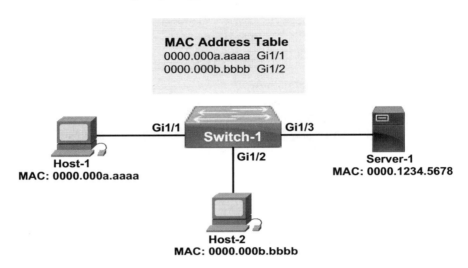

### Example 2:

Refer to the drawing where Host-2 has sent a packet to Server-1. The switch will examine source and destination MAC address of the frame arriving on port Gi1/2 from Host-2. The MAC address table has no entry for either MAC address. The switch will then add the source MAC address (Host-2) to the MAC table. In addition the switch will unicast flood (MAC learning) the frame out all ports except the port where the frame was learned from (Gi1/2). Server-1 with the matching destination MAC address receives the frame and sends a frame to the switch. The switch updates the MAC address table with the MAC address of Server-1.

- **0000.000b.bbbb** is added to the MAC address table
- frame is forwarded out all active switch ports except port Gi1/2

**Figure 2** Frame Switching Topology 2

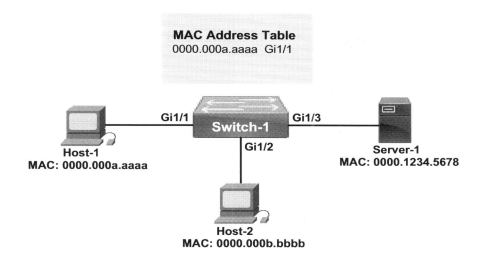

## Example 3:

Refer to the drawing where Host-2 has sent a packet to Server-1. Switch-1 will examine the incoming frame from Host-2 arriving on port Gi1/2. The switch will do a MAC table lookup based on the destination MAC address. The switch determines the destination MAC address is assigned to Server-1. The frame is forwarded to port Gi1/3 associated with Server-1.

- switch will examine the frame and MAC address table lookup
- frame is forwarded out switch port Gi1/3

**Figure 3** Frame Switching Topology 3

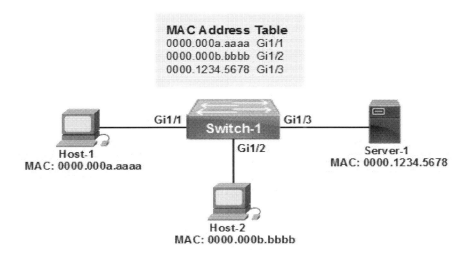

## Ethernet Frame Format

Cyclic Redundancy Check (CRC) is a number (FCS) calculated on each frame received to verify data integrity. The layer 2 frame is discarded if the received FCS number doesn't match the original. It is an error detection technique and not error recovery. Any error detection and/or error recovery is managed by transport layer 4 protocols. The source MAC address (SA) and destination MAC address (DA) are 6 bytes. The following are the fields that comprise an Ethernet frame.

- preamble
- source MAC address (6 bytes)
- destination MAC address (6 bytes)
- type/length
- payload (variable)
- FCS

## Ethernet Frame

Ethernet Header = 18 bytes

| Source MAC Address | Destination MAC Address | Type | Payload | FCS |
|---|---|---|---|---|
| 6 bytes | 6 bytes | 2 bytes | 46-1500 bytes | 4 bytes |

## Access Ports (data and voice)

Cisco switch ports supports access mode or trunk mode. The port mode is configured when enabling the interface. The standard Layer 2 switch port is referred to as an access port. Switch access ports that receives a packet with an 802.1q tag in the header will discard the packet without learning the source MAC address.

The access port connects access devices such as a hosts, servers and wireless access points. The switch port can only be assigned one VLAN unless you are connecting an IP phone. The data VLAN and voice VLAN is permitted on an access port with the following configuration commands.

switch(config)# **interface fastethernet0/1**
switch(config-if)# **switchport mode access** *(configure access port mode)*
switch(config-if)# **switchport access vlan 9** *(assign vlan 9 to data traffic)*
switch(config-if)# **switchport voice vlan 10** *(assign vlan 10 to voice traffic)*

The following commands list all VLANs configured on a switch.

>    switch# **show vlan**
>    switch# **show vlan brief**

The following command is used to verify switch port/s assigned to a single VLAN.

>    switch# **show vlan id** [vlan]

## Trunk Interface

The purpose of a switch trunk is to forward multiple VLANs between switches. The switch port must be configured for trunk mode to enable forwarding of multiple VLANs. That allows communication between hosts assigned to the same VLAN that spans switches. Forwarding multiple VLANs across a switch link requires trunk mode to enable the VLAN tagging feature. The following configures a switch trunk interface with native VLAN 999 and allow VLANs 10-12

>    switch(config-if)# **switchport mode trunk**
>    switch(config-if)# **switchport trunk native vlan 999**
>    switch(config-if)# **switchport trunk allowed vlan 10-12**

## 802.1q VLAN Tag

802.1q protocol has a 12 bit VLAN ID field used to identify VLAN membership of a frame. The switch adds a 4-byte tag to each Ethernet frame for VLAN membership. The Ethernet frame header is modified as a result of adding the VLAN tag. That requires recalculation of the FCS value used for CRC. Switch access ports that receives a packet with an 802.1q tag in the header will discard the packet without learning source MAC address.

- open standard for multi-vendor switch connectivity
- default setting for Cisco switches
- provide VLAN tagging across a switch trunk

## Native VLAN

The native VLAN is used to forward control traffic across a switch trunk. Changing the native VLAN from VLAN 1 to any available nondefault VLAN is a Cisco security best practice. There are security vulnerabilities associated with the default VLAN 1. In addition STP issues are minimized by selecting a nondefault VLAN instead of VLAN 1. Control traffic (CDP, PAgP, VTP, STP and DTP) always uses VLAN 1 and travel on the native VLAN (untagged traffic) by default.

The trunk tags all data VLANs for identification purposes. The untagged traffic is separated from data traffic as a result. None of the control traffic except STP and DTP are forwarded across the native VLAN when the native VLAN is changed to a nondefault value. STP and DTP are management protocols that must be untagged across trunk links.

The native VLAN configured on a trunk link must match between switches to forward untagged packets across the trunk correctly. VLAN hopping is a security vulnerability caused by native VLAN mismatch. STP and DTP can detect native VLAN mismatches.

## VLAN Pruning

The purpose of VLAN pruning is to permit or deny VLANs across a switch trunk. The Cisco default is to allow all VLANs across the trunk. The local switch alerts the neighbor switch of all local VLANs that are not active (not configured). Any VLANs that are not configured are pruned by the neighbor switch to minimize unicast, broadcast and multicast traffic across the trunk. The Cisco default configuration is to allow all VLANs from the range 1 - 4094 across the trunk.

The network administrator can add or remove VLANs after that command is issued based on requirements. Specify multiple non-consecutive VLANs with commas or a hyphen to specify a range of consecutive VLANs. The following interface command will **only allow** VLAN 10, VLAN 11 and VLAN 12 across the trunk.

> switch(config-if)# **switchport trunk allowed vlan 10-12**

The **add | remove** keyword only applies after pruning has already occurred on the trunk interface to limit the initial default VLANs allowed from the range 1-4094.

> switch(config-if)# **switchport trunk allowed vlan add** [vlan id, vlan id, ...]

The following interface command will remove VLAN 10 from the trunk. That will filter all traffic from that VLAN so it cannot traverse the trunk link between switches.

> switch(config-if)# **switchport trunk allowed vlan remove 10**

The following interface command will add VLAN 12 to the trunk interface. That will permit all traffic from that VLAN so it can traverse the trunk link between switches.

> switch(config-if)# **switchport trunk allowed vlan add 12**

## Dynamic Trunking Protocol

- DTP enables dynamic negotiation of a trunk between two switches
- DTP is Cisco proprietary protocol only
- DTP modes are **nonegotiate**, **desirable** and **auto**.
- DTP **auto** mode is enabled by default on switch ports
- There is no trunk negotiated with the default DTP mode setting

DTP request frames are sent to the neighbor switch to negotiate the trunk setup. The switch port configured with **desirable** or **auto** mode listen for DTP requests. The switch port configured with **desirable** mode actively sends DTP frames to establish a trunk with neighbor switch.

DTP provides dynamic negotiation based on the mode setting where at least one of the interfaces is configured with **desirable** mode. The switch interface configured with **switchport mode trunk** command is a static trunk with **on** mode.

The following describe the operation of each switch port configuration:
- switchport mode access = access port only (no trunk)
- switchport mode trunk = trunk statically formed and no DTP frames sent
- switchport mode dynamic auto = listens for DTP requests
- switchport mode dynamic desirable = listens and sends DTP requests
- switchport nonegotiate = disable DTP

**Table 22**  Dynamic Trunking Protocol Modes

| Switch-1 | Switch-2 | Result |
| --- | --- | --- |
| auto | auto | access port |
| auto | desirable | trunk |
| auto | on | trunk |
| desirable | on | trunk |
| desirable | desirable | trunk |
| nonegotiate | nonegotiate | access port |
| nonegotiate | on | trunk |
| on | access | access port |
| on | on | trunk |

Table 22 describe how switch modes affects trunk setup between switches. DTP **auto** mode supports access mode and trunk mode. The neighbor incoming negotiation would determine whether the switch port operation is access or trunk. The **nonegotiate** mode is configured on both switch interfaces that do not support DTP mode or should not establish trunking. DTP frames are sent at one second intervals during negotiation and every 30 seconds after that.

The following are methods for disabling DTP on a switch interface:
- switchport nonegotiate
- switchport mode access
- static trunk mode

## Normal/Extended VLANs

Cisco switch ports are assigned to VLAN 1 as a default configuration. VLAN 1 is used for management traffic and cannot be deleted. The normal range that include VLAN range 2 - 1001 can be added, modified or deleted from the switch. Cisco recommends assigning all data and voice traffic to a non-default VLAN.

**Table 23** VLAN Usage

| VLAN Range | Description |
|---|---|
| VLAN 1 – 1005 | normal VLAN range |
| VLAN 1006 - 4094 | extended VLAN range |
| VLAN 1, 1002 - 1005 | auto-created and cannot be deleted |
| VLAN 1006 - 4094 | cannot be pruned from a trunk |

## VLAN Trunking Protocol (VTP)

- VTP enable VLAN configuration automatically across multiple switches
- VTP enables synchronization of VLANs between subnets
- VTP modes are client, server and transparent
- VTP default mode for switch is server mode

VTP Requirements

- configure all switch uplink ports as trunk interfaces
- designate at least one VTP server per domain
- configure all switches with the same VTP domain name and password
- switch must be in VTP server or transparent mode to permit configuring VLANs on the local switch

VTPv2 Enhancements

- Token Ring VLANs
- VLAN consistency check
- transparent mode forwards VTP advertisements with no version check

Configure VTP server mode with password *ccnalab* and VTP domain name *cisco*.

switch(config)# **vtp mode server**
switch(config)# **vtp password ccnalab**
switch(config)# **vtp domain cisco**

# EtherChannel

EtherChannel bundles multiple physical switch links between switches into a single logical link. It is sometimes referred to as switch port aggregation. The advantages include fault tolerance (redundancy) and high speed connectivity between switches. There is static configuration (on/on) that explicity creates an EtherChannel.

There is dynamic negotiation of EtherChannel with PAgP and LACP protocols. The mode assigned to local switch port and neighbor switch port determine whether an EtherChannel is created. Cisco switches support assigning a maximum eight ports to a single Etherchannel bundle.

PAgP is the Cisco proprietary protocol and auto mode is the default mode when enabled. LACP is an open standard with passive as default mode. It supports a maximum sixteen ports however only eight ports can be active simultaneously. The additional LACP ports are used for failover purposes only. The interface is assigned to channel and protocol mode configured with the **channel-group** command for each protocol. The port channel logical interface is assigned a number to match the channel group number. The speed, duplex and VLAN setting must match for all ports members assigned to an EtherChannel.

**Table 24** PAgP Modes

| Switch-1 | Switch-2 | Result |
|---|---|---|
| on | auto | err-disable |
| on | desirable | err-disable |
| auto | auto | none |
| auto | desirable | etherchannel |
| desirable | desirable | etherchannel |

**Table 25** LACP Modes

| Switch-1 | Switch-2 | Result |
|---|---|---|
| on | active | err-disable |
| on | passive | err-disable |
| passive | passive | none |
| active | passive | etherchannel |
| active | active | etherchannel |

Configure PAgP desirable mode on a switch port and assign to channel group 1.

>switch(config)# **switchport mode access**
>switch(config)# **switchport access vlan 10**
>switch(config)# **duplex auto**
>switch(config)# **speed auto**
>switch(config)# **channel-group 1 mode desirable**

Configure LACP active mode on a switch port and assign to channel group 1.

>switch(config)# **switchport mode access**
>switch(config)# **switchport access vlan 10**
>switch(config)# **duplex auto**
>switch(config)# **speed auto**
>switch(config)# **channel-group 1 mode active**

## Spanning Tree Protocol

Spanning Tree is deployed to prevent Layer 2 loops and broadcast storms where frames are forwarded in a loop between switches. The most current STP protocol supports per VLAN instances (PVST+). Redundant topologies are characterized by multiple paths that could cause Layer 2 loops. STP forwards and block specific ports to eliminate forwarding loops between switches. Some possible problems that can occur when configuring redundant links between switches:

- multiple copies of unicast frames
- broadcast storm flooding
- MAC address table instability

STP creates a loop free Layer 2 topology by enabling some switch ports to forward traffic and some to block traffic. That is based on electing a root bridge. The switch with the lowest bridge ID is elected root bridge. The bridge ID is comprised of priority setting and MAC address. STP calculates lowest path cost for each neighbor interface to the root bridge. The neighbor switch port that receives the best BPDU (least cost to the root bridge) is assigned root port for that switch.

BPDU is an STP message that is sent between switches. The hello timer setting is the interval between BPDU advertisements. The BPDU message contains STP information from the sending switch. That includes STP timers, root bridge ID, sender bridge ID and port (path) cost. The following are four STP port states defined with 802.1d original standard.

- blocking
- listening
- learning = populating MAC address table
- forwarding

The newer 802.1w (RSTP) standard is comprised of three port states. They include discarding, learning and forwarding. The discarding state is new and equivalent to the blocking and listening states of older 802.1d protocol. The single RSTP discarding state enables faster convergence. RPVST+ is based on RSTP and includes separate STP instances for each VLAN enabled on a switch.

## Root Bridge Selection

The default priority of a Cisco switch is 32768. STP selects the root bridge (switch) with the lowest priority. The switch with the lowest bridge ID is elected when all switches have the same priority. The bridge ID is calculated from the priority setting and MAC address. The switch with the lowest MAC address becomes the root bridge as a result. The Spanning Tree election assigns root bridge along with designated ports, root ports and alternate ports to neighbor switches. The root port is a switch port on a neighbor switch that has the least cost path to the root bridge. It is a primary forwarding link to the root bridge. STP operational status is available with **show spanning-tree summary** command.

## PortFast

Spanning Tree Protocol (STP) enhancements are designed to optimize network convergence. The access layer connects hosts on single point-to-point connection where Layer 2 loops do not occur. PortFast is enabled on switch ports where hosts and wireless access points are connected. That allows the switch ports to transition from disabled or blocking state to forwarding state immediately on startup.

## BPDU guard

The purpose of BPDU guard is to err-disable (shutdown) an access switch port when BPDUs are received from a network device. BPDU guard is enabled on an access switch port where hosts or wireless devices connect. BPDU guard is configured on switch port to prevent devices from affecting the STP topology. Connecting a new switch to your cubicle jack would trigger an STP recalculation. The new switch is now connected to an access switch port causing a Layer 2 topology change notification. The result could include a new root bridge election.

## Cisco Discovery Protocol (CDP)

CDP is a Layer 2 Cisco proprietary neighbor discovery protocol. Cisco IP phone appears to CDP as a unique neighbor device with an IP address. During bootup, the IP phone receives voice VLAN configuration from the access switch port.

- CDP is enabled by default both globally and on all network interfaces
- CDP update timer = 60 seconds (default)
- CDP is enabled globally by default on Cisco devices and interfaces
- CDP can be re-enabled CDP globally with **cdp run** global command
- CDP can be re-enabled per interface with **cdp enable** interface level command

## Link Layer Discovery Protocol (LLDP)

LLDP is an open standard network discovery protocol specified with IEEE 802.1ab standard for multi-vendor environments. The network devices share identity and functionality via LLDP and with neighbors.

- The default packet update interval for LLDP is 30 seconds.

- Network interfaces with LLDP enabled advertise default TLV attributes of chassis ID, port ID and TTL.

- Cisco IP phones are enabled for LLDP when LLDP packets are first sent from the phone to the switch.

- Global configuration command **lldp run** enables LLDP globally

- Interface level configuration command **lldp receive** enables an interface to receive LLDP packets.

# Routing Technologies

## Router Operation

Routers are primarily responsible for logical addressing and best path selection between different subnets. Routers make forwarding decisions based on the destination subnet (prefix). The router will do a routing table lookup then rewrite the source and destination MAC address in the frame header.

They build a routing table with route entries comprised of route, metric and next hop address. The router selects the route based on longest match rule and forwards packets to the next hop router (neighbor). There is support for load balancing, flow control and error recovery as well. Each packet has a source IP address and destination IP address. The router does a routing table lookup for a route to the destination subnet. The packet is then forwarded to the next hop address associated with the selected route.

## Frame Rewrite

The source and destination MAC address are updated by routers as frames are forwarded between routers. The source MAC address is the router egress interface and destination MAC address is the neighbor ingress interface. The forwarding decisions for routers are based on destination IP address and not destination MAC address. The source and destination IP address do not change between source and destination hosts. Any Layer 3 device such as a host or a router will write an IP header to create a packet with the source IP address and destination IP address.

## Time-to-Live (TTL)

The IP header has a field called Time-to-Live (TTL) that has a default value of 255. The purpose of TTL is to prevent packets from infinitely looping as a result of a routing loop. The TTL field is decremented by one with each router hop. That guarantees the packet will be discarded after 255 hops.

## Routing Table Lookup

The router selects routes to install in the routing table. Sometimes there are multiple routes from multiple routing protocols to the same destination. The administrative distance of a route determines the route installed in the routing table. The longest match rule selects the route with the longest subnet mask (prefix) from routes in the routing table. The metric is used to select best path to destination and where multiple paths exist.

- lowest administrative distance
- longest match (subnet mask)
- lowest metric (cost)

## ARP Operation

ARP is a network protocol that resolves a known IP address to an unknown MAC address. The local host must know the MAC address of the remote host before packets can be sent. The host sends an ARP request to the default gateway if there is no local ARP entry. The default gateway (router) sends a proxy ARP broadcast and returns the MAC address for a server to the host. The switches note the server MAC address as well and update their MAC address table.

## Route Selection

The router does a routing table lookup for the best route to the destination subnet. It is used for packet forwarding to the destination subnet. The router builds a routing table with multiple routes (prefixes). The routes are assigned an administrative distance and metric cost. The administrative distance (AD) is a value based on the route source (type) and used by the router to select what route is installed in the routing table. AD is the tie breaker for routes with the same subnet (prefix) mask length to the same destination. The directly connected route with AD = 0 is considered the most reliable among routes to the same destination.

Metric is a path cost assigned to a specific route. **The administrative distance and metric assigned to a route will determine what route is installed in the routing table**. The router installs the route with the lowest administrative distance including connected, static and default routes. Equal cost load balancing is enabled when the route metrics to the same destination are equal. EIGRP routing protocol supports equal and unequal load balancing.

Administrative distance is configurable as well to influence route selection. For example a floating static route has a higher AD than a normal static route. It is not installed in the routing table unless the static route with same destination is removed for some reason. The floating static route is installed over a dynamic route if the dynamic route has a higher AD. The route with the lowest metric is installed when there are multiple routes from the **same** routing protocol to the **same** destination. In this example, internal EIGRP has the lowest administrative distance and would be installed in the routing table.

- OSPF: 172.16.1.0/24
- RIPv2: 172.16.1.0/24
- **EIGRP: 172.16.1.0/24**

The following is an example of multiple routes from different routing protocols with different subnet mask (prefix) lengths. As a result they are all considered to be different destinations and all are installed in the routing table.

- OSPF: 172.16.1.0/21
- RIPv2: 172.16.1.0/23
- EIGRP: 172.16.1.0/27

*Packet Forwarding:*

The subnet length is only considered when selecting from multiple routes to the same destination already installed in the routing table. It is commonly referred to as the longest match rule. The longest match rule is used to **select a route already installed in the routing table** as a forwarding decision. Each route has a specific prefix (subnet mask) length. The route with the longest prefix is selected from multiple routes within the same subnet range (destination).

The following is a list of routes installed in the routing table. The router would select 192.168.1.0/28 based on the longest match rule for packet forwarding to destination subnet 192.168.1.10/30

    A. 192.168.1.0/24

    B. 192.168.1.0/26

    **C. 192.168.1.0/28**

    D. 192.168.1.0/25

*Packet Discard*

The router does a lookup for any route to the destination subnet that exists in the routing table. That includes any dynamic, static, default or directly connected route. The packet is discarded when no route exists and a destination unreachable ICMP message is sent to the host.

**Table 26** Administrative Distance (AD)

| Route Source | AD |
|---|---|
| Directly Connected | 0 |
| Static Route | 1 |
| External BGP | 20 |
| EIGRP | 90 |
| OSPF | 110 |
| RIPv2 | 120 |

**Table 27** Distance Vector vs Link State Protocols

| Routing Protocol | Characteristics |
|---|---|
| OSPF | <ul><li>link-state</li><li>metric = link cost (bandwidth)</li><li>global view database topology table</li><li>shortest path to destination calculated</li><li>event-triggered routing updates</li><li>auto-summary disabled (default)</li><li>scalable to large enterprise domains</li><li>faster convergence than RIPv2</li><li>load balancing 4 equal paths</li></ul> |
| EIGRP | <ul><li>distance vector</li><li>metric = bandwidth and delay (distance)</li><li>only neighbor links are known</li><li>best path = lowest distance to destination</li><li>only route changes sent to neighbors</li><li>auto-summary disabled (IOS 15+)</li><li>medium and large network domains</li><li>fastest convergence time</li><li>load balancing 4 equal or unequal paths</li><li>split horizon / route poisoning loop prevention</li></ul> |
| RIPv2 | <ul><li>distance vector</li><li>metric = hop count (distance)</li><li>only neighbor links are known</li><li>best path = least number of hops to destination</li><li>regular full routing table updates to neighbors</li><li>auto-summary enabled (default)</li><li>not scalable</li><li>preferred for smaller network domains</li><li>slow convergence</li><li>load balancing 6 equal paths</li><li>split horizon / route poisoning loop prevention</li></ul> |

## OSPF Operation

- OSPF process ID is a unique number (1 – 65535) assigned to an OSPF routing instance and only locally significant to router.

- There is a separate OSPF topology database for each process ID.

- Any OSPF interface can only be assigned to a single process ID.

- OSPF sends hello packets to neighbors on the same segment (subnet)

- All areas must be connected directly to the backbone (area 0). The virtual link connects an area to the backbone area through an already connected area as transit. It is a hierarchical topology that efficiently minimizes traffic.

- OSPF default hello timer interval for an Ethernet network is 10 seconds. The dead timer is a default of 4 times the hello interval (40 seconds).

- There is no maximum hop count for OSPF so it is unlimited.

- Router ID is manually configured or default to highest loopback IP address

- OSPF passive interfaces are enabled on interfaces connected to neighbors that are not assigned to an OSPF area. That prevents OSPF hello packets that send routing updates. In addition it minimizes security risks and bandwidth utilization on links to non-OSPF neighbors.

OSPF is a classless routing protocol and wildcard masks are required to define subnets for advertising. OSPF **network area** command enable OSPF routing on local interfaces that are assigned an address within the subnet range specified. The routes are advertised to the area assigned. The following command will advertise 192.168.100.0 subnet (route) from any local interface assigned within that same subnet to all connected OSPF neighbors in area 0.

    router(config-router)# **network 192.168.100.0 0.0.0.255 area 0**

OSPFv2 multi-area global configuration that is advertising subnet 192.168.0.0/24 to area 0 and 172.16.1.0/24 to area 1.

    router(config)# **router ospf 1**
    router(config-router)# **router-id 172.16.1.255**
    router(config-router)# **network 192.168.0.0 0.0.255.255 area 0**
    router(config-router)# **network 172.16.1.0 0.0.0.255 area 1**

**Table 28** OSPF Operational Commands

| Command | Description |
|---|---|
| show ip ospf database | display all link states for each area where router has an interface and advertising routers |
| show ip ospf neighbors | display all neighbors that have adjacency with local router and DR |
| show ip ospf interface | display operational state of OSPF enabled interface, timers. process ID and router ID |

## OSPFv3

OSPFv3 neighbors do not have to share the same subnet to form an adjacency. OSPFv3 neighbor adjacency is established with link-local address. OSPFv3 routing is per link instead of per subnet with multiple instances per link support.

- multiple IPv6 addresses per interface
- adjacencies over link-local IP address
- IPv4 and IPv6 addressing
- FF02::5 (all OSPF SPF routers) / FF02::6 (all DR/BDR routers)

The following configuration enables a router interface for OSPFv3 and assigns it to area 0. There are two global commands that enable OSPFv3 for the router. The OSPFv3 global process is assigned to process ID 1 for this example. The interface is enabled when it is assigned to process ID 1 and area 0.

```
router(config)# ipv6 router ospf 1
router(config)# router-id 192.168.1.1

router(config)# interface gigabitethernet0/0
router(config-if)# no ip address
router(config-if)# ipv6 enable
router(config-if)# ipv6 address 2001:AB3E::/64 eui-64
router(config-if)# ipv6 ospf 1 area 0
```

## EIGRP Operation

- EIGRP routers only advertise routes within the same autonomous system (AS). AS number assigned to each connected interface must match.

- There is less CPU processing required for single AS design and route propagation is automatic within single EIGRP AS (instance).

- The **variance** command allows for unequal cost load balancing between EIGRP enabled interfaces. The default is to forward traffic across the link with the lowest metric when there are multiple links to the same destination.

## EIGRP Timers

- EIGRP interfaces sends hello packets to all EIGRP neighbors at 5 second intervals (default) and is configurable.

- default holddown timer interval is when three hello packets (15 seconds) are not received from an EIGRP neighbor interface.

- holddown timer is the time interval that router waits before declaring the neighbor unreachable, neighbor adjacency dropped and goodbye message

- holddown timer configuration affects network convergence after link failure.

**Table 29** EIGRP Routing Tables

| EIGRP Table | Description |
|---|---|
| Neighbor | directly connected EIGRP neighbors with adjacency established |
| Topology | routes learned from each neighbors including feasible successors |
| Routing | best (successor) routes selected from the EIGRP topology table |

* Feasible successors are backup routes stored in the topology table.

EIGRP **network** command enable EIGRP routing on local interfaces that are assigned an address within the subnet range specified. The routes are advertised to the EIGRP autonomous system (AS) assigned to the interface. AS number assigned to each router must match to form neighbor adjacencies. The following command will advertise 172.16.1.0/24 subnet (route) from any local interface assigned within that same subnet to all connected EIGRP neighbors in AS 10.

    router(config)# **router eigrp 10**
    router(config-router)# **network 172.16.1.0 0.0.0.255**

There is support for classless routing with **no auto-summary** command where required. There is no wildcard mask required when advertising EIGRP classful subnets. Consider for example **network 172.16.0.0** command would advertise all 172.16.0.0/16 subnets. It is the default (classful) subnet mask for that class B address. The following is an example configuration of classful subnets. The classful subnets advertised include 192.168.0.0/24 and 172.16.0.0/16 to AS 1.

>router(config)# **router eigrp 1**
>router(config-router)# **network 192.168.0.0**
>router(config-router)# **network 172.16.3.0**

**Table 30** EIGRP Operational Commands

| Command | Description |
| --- | --- |
| show ip eigrp topology | display all feasible successor routes and DUAL states for destination route computation |
| show ip eigrp neighbors | display all neighbors that have adjacency with local router and routing metrics |
| show ip eigrp interfaces | display all EIGRP enabled interfaces and routing performance |

## EIGRP for IPv6

The subnets assigned to the local interfaces are advertised when EIGRP is enabled on an interface. The **router-id** command is only required when there are no IPv4 interfaces configured on the router. EIGRP for IPv6 includes the following features:

- EIGRP is enabled per interface
- no support for global network statements
- protocol instance is not enabled until the router ID configured
- router ID is a 32-bit decimal value

The following example enables EIGRP for IPv6 globally on a router and advertises IPv6 subnet address assigned to interface in autonomous system 1.

>router(config)# **ipv6 unicast-routing**
>router(config)# **router-id 172.16.1.1**
>router(config)# **interface gigabitethernet0/0**
>router(config-if)# **ipv6 address 2001:DB8:3C4D:2::1/64**
>router(config-if)# **no shut**
>router(config-if)# **ipv6 enable**
>router(config-if)# **ipv6 eigrp 1**
>router(config-if)# **ipv6 router eigrp 1**

## RIPv2 for IPv4

The primary enhancement to RIPv2 over RIPv1 is support for classless routing updates. That enables route advertisements that include the subnet mask (prefix) length. RIPv2 routes use MD5 authentication between routers for security. RIPv2 sends routing table updates as a multicast to 224.0.0.9 instead of a broadcast used with RIPv1. The same hop count (metric) of 15 is unchanged for RIPv2.

RIPv2 **network** command enable RIPv2 routing on local interfaces that are assigned an address within the subnet range specified. The **network** statement however only supports classful subnets as a default configuration with no subnet mask or wildcard mask. RIPv2 would change **network 172.16.1.0** to **network 172.16.0.0** and advertise only 172.16.0.0/16 subnet to RIPv2 neighbors. There is support for classless routing with **no auto-summary** command. RIPv2 would then advertise 172.16.1.0/24 subnet (route) from any local interface assigned within that same subnet to all connected RIPv2 neighbors.

RIPv2 globally enabled on router-1 and advertising 172.33.2.0, 192.168.1.0 and 192.168.3.0 subnets. Advertise a default route to all peering RIPv2 neighbors and turn off automatic summarization to enable classless routing.

    router(config)# **router rip**
    router(config-router)# **version 2**
    router(config-router)# **network 172.33.2.0**
    router(config-router)# **network 192.168.1.0**
    router(config-router)# **network 192.168.3.0**
    router(config-router)# **default-information originate**
    router(config-router)# **no auto-summary**

## Route Summarization

Any routing protocol that summarizes routes will advertise classful subnets only based on the address class. The routing protocol would summarize 172.16.100.0 to 172.16.0.0/16 and advertise that to neighbors. The default subnet mask for any class B address is 255.255.0.0 (/16) classful mask. The **no auto-summary** command is configured on to enable classless routing updates.

**Table 31** Route Summarization

| route prefix | address class | auto-summary |
|---|---|---|
| 192.168.200.0/24 | class C | 192.168.200.0/24 |
| 172.33.10.0/24 | class B | 172.33.0.0/16 |
| 200.200.1.32/27 | class C | 200.200.1.0/24 |
| 10.10.100.0/16 | class A | 10.0.0.0/8 |

## Dynamic Route

There are various routing protocols that are designed to exchange route information with neighbors. The network administrator does not configure dynamic routes. They are learned so that each router installs and selects routes for best path selection. Connected routes (subnet prefixes) are added based on local network interface addressing. The router installs a corresponding local host route (/32) as well for each connected interface.

## Static Route

The static route is more specific than a default route. The static route says – *to reach destination subnet 172.16.1.0/24 forward packets to next hop address 172.16.12.1 or exit interface Serial0/1*. Static routes are required at both routers as well to route (forward) in both directions when no routing protocols are enabled. The advantages are added security with manual routes and less advertisements when compared with dynamic routing protocols.

      router(config)# ip route 172.16.1.0 255.255.255.0 172.16.12.1
      router(config)# ip route 172.16.1.0 255.255.255.0 Serial0/1

## Floating Static Route

The static route configured with a higher administrative distance than a dynamic route or static route is a floating static route. It is installed in the routing table only when the currently selected route is not available. That could result from a link failure for example. The floating static route is typically configured to forward traffic across a backup link. The static route has a lower administrative distance compared with the floating static route and selected as the primary route. The floating static route with the higher administrative distance **200** becomes active only when the primary static route is not available.

      router(config)# ip route 192.168.3.0 255.255.255.0 192.168.2.1 **200**

## Default Route

The default route is referred to as gateway of last resort packet forwarding. Any route, where no match exists, is forwarded to the next hop IP address specified with the default route. The default route says – *forward all traffic to next hop address of 172.16.1.1 when no route to the destination exists in the routing table*. The default route is often configured to forward packets to the internet. In addition they minimize route advertisements when compared with dynamic routes. The administrative distance of default and static routes is one.

      router(config)# ip route 0.0.0.0 0.0.0.0 172.16.1.1

## Default-Information Originate

The purpose of default-information originate is to advertise a default route to connected neighbors. There is a single route configured under a dynamic routing protocol. It is advertised to all neighbors that have the same routing protocol enabled. The traditional default route is configured locally on a router and used as a gateway of last resort. It is often deployed as a backup solution to a primary link.

## IPv6 Static Routing

IPv6 static route to destination subnet 2001:DB8:3C4D:1::/64

    router(config)# **ipv6 unicast-routing**
    router(config)# **ipv6 route 2001:DB8:3C4D:1::/64  2001:DB8:3C4D:2::1**

IPv6 default route with next hop of 2001:DB8:3C4D:2::1

    router(config)# **ipv6 unicast-routing**
    router(config)# **ipv6 route ::/0  2001:DB8:3C4D:2::1**

## Routing Table Components

Each routing table is comprised of multiple routes with the following attributes.

1. Routing protocol code is the route source (type).
2. Route prefix is the destination subnet.
3. Administrative distance is the trustworthiness of the route source.
4. Metric is the path cost to the destination subnet.
5. Next hop is the interface of a neighbor router specified with a route.
6. Local interface is the exit interface used to forward packet to next hop adder
7. Age is the amount of time the route has been installed

### *Example*

O    192.168.12.236/30 [110/128] via 192.168.12.233, 00:35:36, Serial0/0

- Routing protocol code = O (OSPF)
- Destination subnet (prefix) = 192.168.12.236/30
- Administrative distance = 110
- Metric = 128
- Next hop address = 192.168.12.233
- Local exit interface = Serial0/0
- Age = 00:35:36

**Table 32** Routing Source Codes

| Route Source | Protocol Code |
|---|---|
| EGP | E |
| EIGRP | D |
| Host (/32) | L |
| Connected | C |
| OSPF | O |
| Default Route | S* |
| Static Route | S |

## InterVLAN Routing

Layer 3 routing services are required to route packets between hosts assigned to different VLANs. That includes hosts connected to the same or different switches. The most common solution is router-on-a-stick for enabling Inter-VLAN routing. The alternative is a Layer 3 switch configured with SVIs. Layer 2 switches do not route packets. The following steps are required to configure router-on-a-stick.

1. Configure trunk mode on switch uplink to router and allow host VLANs.
2. Configure a subinterface with VLAN encapsulation for each host VLAN.
3. Configure each subinterface with an IP address in the same subnet as host.

### Configuration Example

The following enables a trunk interface and allows host VLAN 10 and VLAN 11

    switch(config)# **switchport mode trunk**
    switch(config)# **switchport trunk allowed vlan 10-11**

The following enables router subinterfaces for host VLAN 10 and VLAN 11 on physical interface gigabitethernet0/0

    router(config)# **interface gigabitethernet0/0.10**
    router(config-subif)# **encapsulation dot1q 10**
    router(config-subif)# **ip address 192.168.10.254 255.255.255.0**
    router(config)# **interface gigabitethernet0/0.11**
    router(config-subif)# **encapsulation dot1q 11**
    router(config-subif)# **ip address 192.168.11.254 255.255.255.0**

## IPv4 Packet

| Version 4-bits | Header Length 4-bits | DSCP 8 bits | ECN 2 bits | Total Length 16 bits | |
|---|---|---|---|---|---|
| | | | | | |

| Version 4-bits | Header Length 4-bits | DSCP 8 bits | ECN 2 bits | Total Length 16 bits |
|---|---|---|---|---|
| Identification 16 bits | | | Flag 3 bits | Fragment Offset 13 bits |
| Time to Live (TTL) 8 bits | Protocol 8 bits | | Header Checksum 16 bit | |
| 32-bit Source IP Address | | | | |
| 32-bit Destination IP Address | | | | |
| Options if Header Length > 5 | | | | |
| Payload (Data) | | | | |

IPv4 Header = 20 bytes

## TCP Segment

| 16-bit Source Port | | | 16-bit Destination Port | |
|---|---|---|---|---|
| 32-bit Sequence Number | | | | |
| 32-bit Acknowledgement Number | | | | |
| Data Offset | 3-bits Reserved | 9-bits Flags | 16-bits Window Size | |
| 16-bit Checksum | | 16-bit Urgent Pointer | | |
| Options and Padding | | | | |
| Payload (Data) | | | | |

TCP Header = 20 bytes

# WAN Technologies

## TCP Handshake

TCP-based applications require a three-way handshake for host-to-server connectivity. The following describes the exchange of messages.

1. host sends TCP SYN message to server with bit set
2. server sends TCP SYN/ACK message to host with bit set for both
3. host sends message to server with TCP ACK bit set

## Point-to-Point Protocol (PPP)

The maximum speed supported on a single PPP link is T1/E1 however MLPPP enables bundling for increased bandwidth. PPP is encapsulation type and must match between peering routers. In addition passwords must match and local username must match peering router.

- LCP establishes, manage and terminates the WAN connection (L2).
- LCP negotiates PAP/CHAP authentication with the remote peer router.
- NCP provides protocol encapsulation for multiple Layer 3 network protocols
- Normal operational status for LCP is *Open* for PPP connection setup.

**Table 33** WAN Access Protocols

| Protocol | Usage |
|---|---|
| SSL VPN | web browser encryption, granular application security |
| MPLS | multiprotocol, labels, ISP managed, IPv4/IPv6, full mesh |
| IPsec VPN | static VPN, private, point-to-point topology, router peering |
| DMVPN | internet-based, Layer 3, cloud connectivity, hub and spoke |
| GRE | DMVPN, routing protocol support, increase hop count |
| Metro Ethernet | Layer 2, bandwidth on demand, distance limits |
| PPPoE | internet-based, Layer 2, DSL, cable, static configuration |

## DMVPN Advantages

- lower support costs and scalability
- tunnel multiple protocols across the internet
- dynamic VPN tunnel setup and configuration
- enable increased security with encryption
- redundant (backup) tunnel connections

**show interface tunnel** [number]

Verify the operational status (up/up) of GRE tunnel and the assigned IP address. In addition the tunnel source address and local interface is shown along with transport configuration.

**Table 34** Quality of Service (QoS)

| Technique | Description |
|---|---|
| congestion avoidance | WRED, tail drop, thresholds |
| bandwidth management | shaping, policing, CAR |
| congestion management | FIFO, WFQ, PQ, CBWFQ (queuing) |
| traffic marking | Class of Service, DHCP, NBAR |
| service-policy | attach policy to interface |

\* DHCP is Layer 3 marking of IP header DSCP field byte (ToS)
\* Class of Service is Layer 2 marking of Ethernet frame 802.1q priority field
\* default trust state for network interfaces is untrusted

## Traffic Shaping vs Policing

The following is a list of features and operation of traffic shaping

- minimize the effect of bandwidth hogging on available network bandwidth.
- shaping does support packet queueing
- queuing prevents packet forwarding from exceeding maximum data rate (CIR)
- shaping limits the maximum data rate on egress interface only
- shape traffic rate lower than maximum speed of physical interface.
- The queuing of packets can affect delay sensitive traffic with higher latency.

The following is a list of features and operation of policing

- policing does not queue packets and that minimizes latency
- policing drops or remarks traffic that exceed thresholds such as CIR
- policing can be applied to ingress and egress interfaces
- no minimum bandwidth guarantee with traffic shaping or policing.

## External BGP (eBGP)

- BGP is a routing protocol with connectivity based on TCP transport
- BGP router ID provides recovery from TCP session collisions
- Router ID is highest loopback IP address by default
- BGP neighbor peering is based on IP address and AS number
- BGP advertises routes based on the static routes and the **network** command
- BGP public AS range is from 1 - 64511
- BGP private AS range is from 64512 – 65535
- eBGP is defined as any peering to a different BGP AS from local AS

### eBGP Configuration Example

- enable BGP with private AS 65535 to local router
- add eBGP peering to neighbor AS 65534
- assign IP address 172.16.1.2 to peering neighbor
- advertise network 10.10.34.1/24 to peering neighbor

    router(config)# **router bgp 65535**
    router(config-router)# **neighbor 172.16.1.2 remote-as 65534**
    router(config-router)# **network 10.10.34.1 mask 255.255.255.0**

### show ip bgp neighbors

Display all BGP peering sessions and TCP connection information. The neighbor configuration listed include the following. Normal BGP state = <u>Established</u> for any BGP peering session.

- router ID
- IP address
- AS number
- neighbor state

### show ip bgp summary

Display all BGP routing information for neighbor connections including path, prefix (subnet) and attribute information.

# Infrastructure Services

**Table 35** DNS Commands

| IOS Command | Description | Example |
|---|---|---|
| ip name-server | IP address of DNS server | 172.16.1.254 |
| ip domain-name | append to unqualified hostnames | cisco.com |
| no ip domain-lookup | disable DNS services | default is enabled |
| ip host | configure static mapping | ip host cisco-s1 200.200.1.1 |

## DHCP Features

- assign and renew IP addresses from a designated pool
- configure TCP/IP address settings on hosts
- IP address is assigned to each host for a fixed lease time
- host sends request that DHCP server renew same IP address
- Ping or Gratuitous ARP is used to detect IP address conflicts
- IP address is removed from pool until conflict is resolved

DHCP request for an IP address:

    Step 1: Server Discovery = DHCPDISCOVERY

    Step 2: IP Lease Offer = DHCPOFFER

    Step 3: IP Lease Request = DHCPREQUEST

    Step 4: IP Lease Acknowledgement = DHCPACK

**show ip dhcp conflict**

Display all IP address conflicts detected on Cisco DHCP server.

**show ip dhcp binding**

Display the IP address and MAC address of DHCP client, lease expiration and assignment type on the IOS DCHP server.

**show ip dhcp pool**

Display the pool range of assigned IP addresses, leased addresses and any pending events.

**Table 36**  Network Time Protocol

| Method | Description |
|---|---|
| ntp peer | backup time server configuration |
| system calendar | initializes software clock after restart |
| software clock | initially set by hardware clock |
| ntp server | external time server polling configuration |
| ntp master | polling of internal time server reference |

## NTP Features

- Provides time source for logging and time stamp transactions
- N+1 server redundancy supported (NTP master + failover)
- Reference is UTC coordinated universal time
- DNS is required for resolving time server IP address
- server mode routers provide time source to client mode devices
- stratum level is the distance from NTP authoritative time source
- server mode routers poll external time server unless **ntp master** enabled
- **show ntp status** displays operational status of NTP server

## Network Address Translation

- conceals private IP address assignments from the internet
- eases management of internet connectivity
- public IP address is assigned by Internet Service Provider
- network address translation is between private and public addressing

### Static NAT

The static NAT translation is a 1:1 configured mapping between local and global addresses. The static translation manually assigns a private IP address to a public IP address. For instance, three public routable IP addresses will allow three static NAT translations. As a result they are a permanent entry in the NAT translation table. They enable a remote host connection from an outside (external) network.

### Dynamic Pool

Dynamic NAT pool mapping translates each private IP address to an available public IP address (1:1) in the NAT pool. The dynamic NAT pool of public IP addresses is shared by all internal IP addresses on a first come first served basis. The maximum number of simultaneous internet connections available is limited to the number of public IP addresses in the NAT pool.

## Port Address Translation

Port Address Translation (PAT) is an IP address translation technique that translates the most internal (private) IP addresses to a single or multiple public IP addresses. It is an enhancement to NAT that assigns a unique source port number to each translated IP address. The host IP address for instance could be identified with 200.200.1.1:10 as the translated source IP address. The 10 is the unique source port making the translated IP address unique. The 16 bit source port field allows for translating 65,535 private (internal) IP addresses.

Configure inside NAT interface

> R1(config)# **interface fastethernet2/0**
> R1(config)# **ip address 192.168.1.3 255.255.255.0**
> R1(config-if)# **ip nat inside**

Configure outside NAT interface

> R1(config)# **interface fastethernet1/0**
> R1(config-if)# **ip address 172.33.1.1 255.255.255.0**
> R1(config-if)# **ip nat outside**

Create pool name *cisco* and assign public address range 172.33.1.1 - 172.33.1.10

> R1(config)# **ip nat pool cisco 172.33.1.1 172.33.1.10 netmask 255.255.255.0**

Configure ACL 100 to permit host IP address range 192.168.0.0 - 192.168.255.255

> R1(config)# **access-list 100 permit ip 192.168.0.0 0.0.255.255 any**

Assign ACL 100 to pool name *cisconet* and enable port address translation

> R1(config)# **ip nat inside source list 100 pool cisconet overload**

## Hot Standby Router Protocol (HSRP)

- creates a single virtual router from at least two routers
- provides a default gateway service to multiple hosts
- share virtual IP address and MAC address
- router with highest priority setting is elected active virtual router
- default priority for a Cisco router is 100
- router with highest IP address is elected when priorities are equal
- preempt command is configured to assign a standby router
- not a routing protocol and virtual IP is not installed in the routing table

Configure HSRP on an interface with local router as active for group 1 and HSRPv2 enabled. In addition enable the virtual IP address of 172.16.1.3 for the HSRP group.

    router(config)# **interface gigabitethernet0/1**
    router(config-if)# **ip address 172.16.1.1 255.255.255.0**
    router(config-if)# **standby version 2** (*enables HSRPv2*)
    router(config-if)# **standby 1 preempt** (*compare priorities for group 1*)
    router(config-if)# **standby 1 priority 110** (*active router*)
    router(config-if)# **standby 1 ip 172.16.1.3** (*virtual IP address*)

# Infrastructure Security

## Device Passwords

**username** [*username*] **privilege** [*level*] **password** [*level*]

    privilege 1 = user EXEC mode (lowest)
    privilege 15 = privileged EXEC mode (highest)
    password 5 = hidden secret password
    password 7 = hidden password

**service password-encryption** = encrypt all passwords in configuration script

**enable password** [*password*] [*level*] = password protect privilege mode
(default privilege level is 15 when not configured with enable command or based on username command)

Configure Telnet login, set the password to *cisco* and a timeout value of 5 minutes for all five default VTY lines

    router(config)# **line vty 0 4**
    router(config-line)# **password cisco**
    router(config-line)# **login**
    router(config-line)# **exec-timeout 5**

Configure console port with password *cisco* for local access security.

    router(config)# **line console 0**
    router(config-line)# **password cisco**
    router(config-line)# **login**

Generate RSA keys for enabling SSH version 2 on a router. SSH version (1 | 2) of host client software is supported by the router when no version is configured.

    router(config)# **crypto key generate rsa**
    router(config)# **ip ssh version 2**
    router(config)# **ip ssh timeout 90 authentication-retries 2**

The following are options for permit / deny of management protocols. Cisco default is to allow all protocols inbound and outbound access on VTY lines.

    device(config-line)# **transport input ssh** *(allow SSH only)*
    device(config-line)# **transport input all** *(allow all protocols)*
    device(config-line)# **transport input telnet ssh** *(allow Telnet and SSH only)*

# Port Security

The purpose of port security is to prevent any unauthorized network device from accessing the corporate network. For instance plugging a laptop from home into the Ethernet jack at work could affect network operations. The switch port enabled with port security would deny access based on the unknown MAC address. Cisco switches support sticky, static or dynamic port security modes.

## Sticky

The **sticky** keyword saves the dynamically learned MAC address to the running configuration script. In addition sticky MAC addresses do not age out of the MAC address table. The switch does have to relearn the MAC addresses after every reboot unless the running configuration is saved to startup configuration file. Removing the **sticky** keyword causes dynamically learned the MAC addresses to persist in the MAC address table only for the connected session. The following IOS commands enable port security on a switch port interface with sticky method.

    switch(config)# **interface fastethernet 0/1**
    switch(config-if)# **switchport port-security**
    switch(config-if)# **switchport port-security mac-address sticky**

## Static

The static option enables a switch interface to only accept frames from a host or network device with a specific MAC address. The static MAC is manually assigned to the switch port and must match to allow frames. The switch port would deny access based on an unknown MAC address. The default setting is to allow only one MAC address per switch port.

    switch(config)# **interface fastethernet 0/1**
    switch(config-if)# **switchport port-security**
    switch(config-if)# **switchport port-security mac-address 0000.1234.5678**

## Dynamic

This is the default setting for port security on a switch interface when it is enabled. The MAC address of the connected host or device is learned dynamically and added to the MAC address table. The MAC address persists in the switch table until switch is powered off or deleted when host is disconnected from the switch.

## Maximum MAC Addresses

The following port security interface command prevent connecting any second host or network device to a switch port. There is support however for allowing multiple MAC addresses to a single switch port. The switch interface can add up to the maximum number of five allowed MAC addresses to the address table.

    switch(config-if)# **switchport port-security maximum 1**

## Violation Actions

There are protect, restrict, shutdown VLAN and shutdown violation modes. The default setting is shutdown where the port shuts down only when the maximum number of secure MAC addresses is exceeded. The switch then sends an SNMP trap notification. Protect mode only sends a security violation notification. There are additional options available with restrict and shutdown VLAN modes.

The security violation could trigger when there is an attempt from a host with a MAC address not in the MAC address table. Duplicate MAC address error cause a violation as well. The restrict mode causes the switch to drop all packets from an unknown source. SNMP trap alerts are sent, syslog messages are logged and the violation counter is incremented.

## Access Control Lists

### Standard ACL

The number range is from 1-99 and 1300-1999. It is comprised of permit or deny statement/s from a source address with a wildcard mask only. The single deny statement requires that you add **permit any** as a last statement for any standard ACL or all packet are denied from all sources.

>   access-list 99 deny host 172.33.1.1
>   access-list 99 permit any

### Standard Named ACL

They are defined with a name instead of number and have the same rules as a standard ACL. The following ACL is named *internet* and will deny all traffic from all hosts connected to 192.168.1.0/24 subnet. It will log any packets that are denied.

>   ip access-list internet log
>   deny 192.168.1.0 0.0.0.255
>   permit any

### Extended Named ACL

They are defined with a name and supports all syntax commands available with extended ACLs. You can dynamically add or delete statements to any named ACL without having to delete and rewrite all lines. They are easier to manage and troubleshoot based on naming conventions. The following named ACL permits http trafic from hosts assigned to 192.168.0.0 subnets access to server 192.168.3.1

>   ip access-list extended http-filter
>   remark permit http to web server
>   permit tcp 192.168.0.0 0.0.255.255 host 192.168.3.1 eq 80
>   permit ip any any

## Extended ACL

The number range is from 100-199 and 2000-2699. It supports multiple permit/deny statements with source / destination IP address or subnet. In addition you can filter on IP, TCP or UDP protocols and destination port. Extended ACL must have a permit all source and destination traffic with **permit ip any any** as a last statement.

Cisco best practices for creating and applying ACLs

- apply extended ACL near source
- apply standard ACL near destination
- order ACL with multiple statements from most specific to least specific
- one ACL can be applied inbound or outbound per interface per Layer 3 protocol
- ACL is applied to an interface with **ip access-group in | out** command

The following are primary differences between IPv4 and IPv6 for ACLs

- IPv6 supports only named ACLs
- IPv6 permits ICMP neighbor discovery (ARP) as implicit default
- IPv6 denies all traffic as an implicit default for the last line of the ACL

### ACL Example 1

The following command permits http traffic from host 10.1.1.1/24 to host 10.1.2.1/24

    access-list 100 permit tcp host 10.1.1.1 host 10.1.2.1 eq 80

The access control list (ACL) statement reads from left to right as - *permit all tcp traffic from source host only to destination host that is http (80)*. The TCP refers to applications that are TCP-based. The UDP keyword is used for applications that are UDP-based such as SNMP for instance.

### ACL Example 2

What is the purpose or effect of applying the following ACL?

    access-list 100 deny ip host 192.168.1.1 host 192.168.3.1
    access-list 100 permit ip any any

The first statement denies **all** application traffic from host-1 (192.168.1.1) to web server (host 192.168.3.1). The *ip* keyword refers to Layer 3 and affects all protocols and applications at layer 3 and higher. The last statement is required to permit all other traffic.

## ACL Example 3

What is the purpose or effect of applying the following ACL?

> access-list 100 permit tcp 192.168.1.0 0.0.0.255 any eq telnet
> access-list 100 permit ip any any

The first statement permits Telnet traffic from all hosts assigned to subnet 192.168.1.0/24 subnet. That include host-1 (192.168.1.1) and host-2 (192.168.1.2). The **tcp** keyword is Layer 4 and affects all protocols and applications at Layer 4 and higher. The **permit tcp** configuration allows the specified TCP application (Telnet). The **any** keyword allows Telnet sessions to any destination host. The last statement is mandatory and required to permit all other traffic.

## ACL Example 4

What is the purpose or effect of applying the following ACL?

> access-list 100 permit ip 172.16.1.0 0.0.0.255 host 192.168.3.1
> access-list 100 deny ip 172.16.2.0 0.0.0.255 any
> access-list 100 permit ip any any

- The first ACL permits only hosts assigned to subnet 172.16.1.0/24 access to all applications on server-1 (192.168.3.1)

- The second statement denies hosts assigned to subnet 172.16.2.0/24 access to either server. That would include any additional hosts added to that subnet and any new servers added.

- The last ACL statement is required to permit all other traffic not matching previous filtering statements.

- ACL is applied to an interface with **ip access-group** command. Most routers often have multiple interfaces (subnets) with hosts assigned. ACL applied outbound to an interface shared by multiple subnets will filter traffic from all hosts for each subnet.

**Table 37** RADIUS vs TACACS

| TACACS+ | RADIUS |
|---|---|
| Cisco proprietary | multi-vendor open standard |
| TCP | UDP |
| separates authentication, authorization and accounting | integrates authentication and authorization |
| encrypts all communication | encrypts passwords only |

# Infrastructure Management

## SNMP

The alert messages generated by SNMP agents include both *Trap* and *Inform*. The purpose of *Trap* messages is to send alerts to the network management station (NMS). For instance, the network device sends a *Trap* to the NMS alerting that a network interface status is down. The *Inform* message is an acknowledgement of a *Trap* to confirm it arrived.

The following are SNMPv3 security enhancements

- message integrity
- authentication
- encryption

SNMPv2 authentication type used is community strings. The following configures SNMP community string to read-only access with password *cisco*. In addition there is a string with read/write access and password *simlabs* for additional rights access.

    switch(config)# **snmp-server community cisco ro**
    switch(config)# **snmp-server community simlabs rw**

## Syslog

The following are correct statements concerning Syslog messaging.

- Syslog provides an external store for system messages
- Syslog messaging is disabled by default
- **service timestamps log datetime localtime** (add timestamp)

The **logging** command enables a Cisco device to log SNMP traps from 0 up to and including level 7. The traps are logged to the Syslog server. The Syslog servers receive informational (6) and lower severity messages as a default.

    router(config)# **logging trap** [level]

Configure a router that will send system messages to a Syslog server that is assigned IP address 192.168.3.1

    router(config)# **logging on**
    router(config)# **logging host 192.168.3.1**
    router(config)# **end**

The **logging facility** command enables you to create separate log files based on message type such as hardware, protocol or module for example. Syslog enables seven logging facilities from local0 to local7. The Cisco default setting for switches and routers is *local7*

**Table 38** Message Logging

| *Level | Message Sent |
|---|---|
| 0 | emergencies |
| 1 | alerts |
| 2 | critical |
| 3 | errors |
| 4 | warnings |
| 5 | notifications |
| 6 | informational |
| 7 | debugging |

* message severity level sends all lower messages as well

**Table 39** Password Recovery

| | |
|---|---|
| Step 1 | Reboot router and press <Ctrl-Break> key to start ROMmon mode |
| Step 2 | Modify the configuration register to prevent the startup configuration file from loading: rommon > **confreg 0x2142** |
| Step 3 | Reboot router and issue the following IOS command: router# **copy startup-config running-config** |
| Step 4 | Change the password and save changes with the following command: router# **copy running-config startup-config** |
| Step 5 | Modify the configuration register with the following command and reboot: router(config)# **config-register 0x2102** |

## Selecting IOS Image on Bootup

1. The device starts and does Power on Self Test (POST) to verify all hardware is operational.

2. The bootstrap loader then determines where to load the IOS image based on the configuration register settings. The default setting loads the first IOS listed with any **boot system** command in the router startup configuration file. The **boot system** command points to a location of an IOS image stored in Flash memory. The file location configured with the first **boot system** command is used when multiple commands exist.

3. The first IOS image listed in Flash memory (where multiple IOS images exist) is loaded when there are no **boot system** commands.

4. IOS is loaded from TFTP server when there is no IOS image on Flash.

5. ROMmon mode starts when there is no IOS image on TFTP server.

## Startup Configuration

The following describes what the Cisco network device does when no startup configuration file is found during bootup. Deleting the startup configuration and restarting the network devices will put the network interfaces in shutdown state.

1. The Cisco network device first attempts to load the startup configuration from NVRAM (default location). There is a copy made of the startup configuration loaded to DRAM for active use. That is referred to as the running configuration.

2. The network device attempts to load the startup configuration file from TFTP server if there is no startup configuration in NVRAM.

3. The network device starts the initial configuration dialog mode if there is no configuration to a TFTP server or it is unavailable. That enables a start from scratch configuration. The preferred method is to restore the most recent startup configuration where available.

    --- System Configuration Dialog ---

    *Would you like to enter the initial configuration dialog?* [yes/no]: **yes**

## Config-Register

0x2100 = Boot from ROM only.

0x2101 = Use the first IOS listed in Flash and ignore any boot system command.

0x2102 = (default) Load the IOS image based on the location specified with the boot system command configured in startup configuration file. Load IOS from Flash if no boot system command is configured. Load the startup configuration file from NVRAM. Ignore the break key and boot to ROM mode if boot fails.

0x2142 = Ignore break key, boot to ROM mode if boot fails and ignore the startup configuration file.

**Table 40** Command Modes

| CLI Mode | Command Prompt |
| --- | --- |
| user EXEC mode | device > |
| privileged EXEC mode | device# |
| global configuration mode | device(config)# |
| ROMmon mode | rommon > |
| routing configuration mode | device(config-router)# |

**Table 41** File Transfer Protocols

| Protocol | Features |
| --- | --- |
| FTP | server-based, username and password logon, TCP |
| SCP | adds encryption (SSH), supports larger files |
| TFTP | server-based, not secure, UDP, single connection |
| USB | fast, network device slot, local copy |

**Table 42** File System Commands

| Command | Description |
| --- | --- |
| show flash | list all files and free memory on Flash (IOS etc.) |
| copy tftp: flash: | copy IOS image file to local Flash memory |
| copy system:running-config ftp \| tftp \| rcp | backup running-config to filesystem ftp \| tftp \| rcp |
| copy nvram:startup-config ftp \| tftp \| rcp | backup startup-config to filesystem ftp \| tftp \| rcp |
| copy tftp: system:running-config | restore running-config from filesystem ftp \| tftp \| rcp |
| copy tftp: nvram:startup-config | restore startup-config from filesystem ftp \| tftp \| rcp |
| erase startup-config | deletes all contents of NVRAM (startup-config etc.) |
| reload | warm restart of network device |
| boot system flash | configure startup-config to boot specific IOS image |
| dir /all | list all files and subdirectories on a filesystem |
| do [command] | run show commands from global config mode |
| terminal monitor | enable sending log messages to the terminal |
| show terminal | display terminal settings for vty lines and protocols |
| show users all | list incoming connections on vty, con and aux |

Default terminal logging settings for Telnet and Console port

- Telnet/SSH logging messages to the terminal are disabled by default
- Console logging messages to the terminal are enabled by default

## Show Version

The output of **show version** command lists the current IOS code version along with feature set license. The command is also available from user mode prompt as well (router >). The following operational and hardware information is listed:

- configuration register settings
- amount of Flash and DRAM memory available
- most recent router power cycle (reboot) method used

## Network Programmability

SDN is an architecture that separates the control plane from the data plane. The purpose is to abstract underlying network infrastructure. That allows network programmability of supported network devices. It is similar to the hypervisor paradigm shift that abstracts (separates) server hardware from software including operating systems, applications and virtual appliances. The same idea is applied to network infrastructure with overlays and programmable services.

SDN Features

- SDN architecture decouples the control and data plane
- control plane is a software module instead of a physical processor
- SDN controller is a centralized control plane with a policy engine
- network infrastructure is abstracted from applications

SDN Controller

- centralized management and network intelligence
- network services are dynamically configurable
- network appears as a single switch
- moves control plane from physical devices to software abstracted layer

The purpose of southbound API provides connectivity between SDN Controller and data plane. The data plane includes the physical and virtual (VM) network devices. The SDN Controller relays information via southbound APIs to network devices. The policy engine is defined at SDN applications where requests are sent via northbound APIs.

The following statements describe SDN APIs

- SDN applications requests are sent via northbound APIs
- SDN Controller relays information via southbound APIs to network devices
- APIC-EM is the Cisco SDN Controller

# Troubleshooting Systems

## OSI Layer Approach

1. Ethernet Cabling
2. Network Interface Card
3. IP Addressing
4. DNS Server
5. Access Control Lists
6. Application Layer

## Host Connectivity

Host TCP/IP address settings are displayed with Windows **ipconfig /all** command output. Network administrator can verify the MAC address and operational status of network interface card (NIC) as well. The following is a list of common points to check when troubleshooting network errors.

- Host TCP/IP settings are correct
- Host is on a common subnet with default gateway assigned to that subnet
- DHCP is enabled for hosts
- Static routes exist in both directions when dynamic routing is not configured
- Any ACL that is filtering application ports

## Operational vs Administrative

Operational status is the running state of a network device. Administrative status is how the device is configured. The operational status confirms for example that an interface is up, switch port mode or routing table entries. They are listed with various IOS show commands from CLI.

## Network Interface States

There is no routing available unless Layer 1 and Layer 2 is working correctly on any network device. The possible interface states for network interfaces are *up/up*, *up/down* and *administratively down / administratively down*. The normal status of an Ethernet interface is up/up. The **shutdown** command would change interface status to *administratively down*. It is not possible to have line protocol in *up* state when the interface (Ethernet) is *down* (down/up).

    Interface = Layer 1, Line protocol = Layer 2

    device# **show interfaces fastethernet1/1**

        *Ethernet 1/1 up, Line Protocol up (normal state)*

Typical Interface Errors

> Layer 1 = cabling, switch configuration mismatches (speed/duplex) errors.
>
> Layer 2 = encapsulation mismatch, spanning tree, clocking errors.

Err-Disabled State

Cisco switch interfaces that are in *err-disabled* state cannot send or receive frames and are essentially shutdown. The cause is either operational or a configuration mismatch. The following are some typical causes of err-disabled state:

- duplex mismatch
- port security violation
- EtherChannel mismatch
- UDLD errors
- BPDU guard
- interface flapping

**Duplex Setting**

Gigabit Ethernet interface supports full-duplex. Traffic can be sent simultaneously in both directions to double the bandwidth available. That eliminates collisions and creates a collision domain per interface. The fact that there are no collisions increase throughput and decreases network latency.

Gigabit Ethernet eliminates collisions unless there is a configuration error or hardware issue. Collisions are caused most often when there is a duplex mismatch on connected interfaces. In addition collisions can occur when there is a bad network interface card (NIC) or cabling error. The switch increments collision counter error after sending 512 bits of a frame. The following are recommended duplex settings to minimize interface errors on network interfaces.

> - configure full-duplex setting on both switch link interfaces
> - configure auto-negotiation on both switch link interfaces

Duplex mismatches with a neighbor interface cause the following interface errors:

- collisions
- input errors
- CRC errors
- slow performance

The cause of collisions on a broadcast domain (VLAN) instead of interfaces are typically the result of duplex mismatches and faulty network interface card (NIC). The most common cause of CRC and runts is collisions. Giant frames result from either a bad NIC card or an MTU configuration error

## Trunking

The following show commands display operational and configuration information for all enabled switch trunk interfaces. It includes both static trunk interfaces or DTP enabled dynamic trunks. There is no support for speed and duplex commands or auto-negotiation with 10 GE ports.

The following are common causes of trunking errors:

- native VLAN mismatch
- access mode configured
- VLAN pruning
- duplex / speed mismatch
- incorrect DTP mode

The following commands display the operational status of trunk interfaces:

> switch# **show interfaces trunk**
> switch# **show interface switchport**

## EtherChannel

The following interface settings must match on all member switch ports assigned to an EtherChannel bundle. The channel-group number (1-48) bundles a port/s to a logical interface or port channel. Gigabit interfaces only support full-duplex traffic.

- duplex half | full | auto
- speed 10 | 100 | 1000 | auto
- protocol (PAgP, LACP or static)
- port mode (access or trunk)
- VLAN membership
- STP configuration
- VLANs allowed (for trunk interfaces)
- Native VLAN (for trunk interfaces)

## VLAN Trunking Protocol (VTP)

- configure all switch uplink ports to trunk mode
- designate at least one VTP server
- configure all switches with the same VTP domain name
- configure all switches with the same domain password
- switch must be in VTP server or transparent mode to configure VLANs

## Managing Switches

Telnet/SSH access requires configuration of a Layer 3 interface on a switch. They connect to switch using the IP address assigned to SVI. The purpose of a default gateway is to forward packets destined for remote subnets to an upstream router.

- The switch is configured with **ip default-gateway** command
- The switch is configured with a Layer 3 VLAN interface (SVI)
- VLAN interface is assigned an IP address for Layer 3 connectivity
- There is an enable password configured on switch
- VTY lines are enabled on switch with a password and login command

## OSPFv2

The following is a list of the most common causes of OSPF network errors. The result is no neighbor adjacency and as a result routes are not advertised.

- interfaces are shutdown
- area ID mismatch between neighbors
- hello and/or dead timer mismatch between neighbors
- OSPF network type mismatch between neighbors
- neighbor interfaces not assigned to the same subnet
- **network** command wildcard mask incorrect
- passive interface enabled on an interface

## EIGRP for IPv4

The following is a list of the most common causes of EIGRP network errors. The result is EIGRP neighbor adjacencies are not formed and routes are not advertised. The network interfaces on point-to-point link are not in the same subnet as required by EIGRP. As a result the routers won't establish EIGRP neighbor adjacency.

- network interface is shutdown
- autonomous system mismatch between neighbors
- K-Value mismatch between neighbor interfaces
- neighbor interfaces are not assigned to the same subnet
- **network** command is missing a subnet
- **network** command is advertising incorrect subnet
- **network** command is configured with incorrect subnet mask
- interface is configured as a passive interface

# EIGRP for IPv6

The following are common causes of EIGRP for IPv6 routing errors. EIGRP for IPv6 requires a router ID to be configured under the routing process. The **router-id** command must be manually configured when IPv4 addressing is unassigned to any interface.

- interface is shutdown
- router ID is not enabled
- EIGRP is not directly configured on interface
- highest IPv4 loopback address is selected then highest IPv4 physical address when router ID it is not manually configured

# RIPv2 for IPv4

The following are some common causes of RIPv2 routing errors.

- interface is shutdown
- directly connected interfaces are not in same subnet
- **network** command has an incorrect subnet address or missing subnet
- **no auto-summary** command is not configured for classless routing

# Inter-VLAN Routing

The following are some common causes of InterVLAN routing errors.

- VLAN encapsulation on subinterface does not match host VLAN
- subnet assigned to subinterface does not match host subnet
- trunk mode is not enabled on switch uplink ports to router
- trunk is pruning and not allowing all host VLANs

# Generic Routing Encapsulation (GRE)

The following are some common causes of GRE tunneling errors.

- incorrect static routes configured to forward packets across tunnel
- no static routes configured to forward packets across tunnel
- private tunnel interfaces are not assigned to the same subnet
- public GRE interfaces are not assigned to the same subnet

## Access Control Lists (ACL)

The following are some common causes of ACL errors.

- missing **permit ip any any** statement
- incorrect order of statements
- incorrect IP address and/or wildcard mask
- incorrect application port number
- incorrect interface or direction applied

## Dynamic Host Configuration Protocol

The following are some common causes of DHCP errors.

- incorrect relay address configured on router
- host is not enabled for DHCP services
- ACL is filtering packets to DHCP server
- misconfigured address pool on DHCP server
- network interface of router not enabled for DHCP client

## Hot Standby Router Protocol

The following are some common causes of HSRP errors.

- virtual IP address must be assigned from same subnet as router interfaces
- all timers must match between HSRP router peers.
- HSRP version (HSRPv1/v2) must match between routers.
- IOS command **show standby** to verify operational status and configuration.

## Network Address Translation

The following are some common causes of NAT errors.

- NAT inside interface unassigned or wrong interface
- NAT outside interface unassigned or wrong interface
- NAT public address pool unassigned or incorrect range
- access list for private host addresses has incorrect wildcard mask
- access list is not assigned to the NAT pool
- overload keyword is not enabled for enabling port address translation

# CCNA SIM Labs

## Troubleshooting Approach

1. Read the question carefully and the reported problem to resolve.

2. Review the network topology drawing.
    - network interfaces
    - subnetting
    - VLANs
    - routing protocol design

3. Access CLI of each switch and router to verify operational status of protocols

    switch# **show ip interface brief**

    → are all enabled interfaces in up/up state?

    → what ip address is assigned to each interface?

    switch# **show vlan**

    → what VLANs are active

    → what are the port assignments?

    switch# **show interfaces trunk**

    → what interfaces are trunking?

    → what is the native VLAN?

    → what VLANs are allowed?

    → is the trunk static or DTP dynamic mode?

    switch# **show etherchannel summary**

    → what ports are members of channel group?

    → what protocol is enabled?

    → does protocol mode enable channel setup?

    → do port settings match between neighbors?

switch# **show vtp status**

- → is VTP enabled?
- → do password and domain name match on switches?
- → are all switch uplinks enabled for trunking?

router# **show ip route**

- → what routes are advertised from neighbors?
- → what routing protocols are enabled
- → what static routes are configured?
- → is there a default route?
- → what routes to neighbors or server/s are missing?
- → what route/s exist to server?
- → how are packets routed to server/s?
- → are there VLAN subinterfaces for Inter-VLAN routing?

router# **show access-lists**

- → what access lists are active?
- → what interface and direction is ACL applied to interface?
- → what hosts, subnets and/or ports are filtered?

4. Analyze the running configuration of each network device to confirm and identify any errors. Review the troubleshooting rules for each protocol and verify with the running configuration. The following command must be issued on all directly connected neighbors to verify that configuration is correct and troubleshoot network connectivity.

device# **show running-config**

<u>Switching</u>

- → is switch port configured for access mode or trunk mode?
- → what VLAN is assigned to an access switch port?
- → are any network interfaces shutdown?
- → what VLANs are allowed across a trunk link?
- → are connected trunk interfaces assigned to same native VLAN
- → does DTP mode of interface enable trunk setup with neighbor?

- → what switch interfaces are members of an etherchannel?
- → does protocol and mode enable etherchannel setup?
- → do local and neighbor port settings match for etherchannel?
- → do switches have the same VTP domain name and password?
- → are switch uplinks configured in trunk mode for VTP domain?
- → SVI (Layer 3 interface) configured for managing switch?

Routing

- → are connected interfaces assigned to the same subnet?
- → what dynamic routing protocols are enabled?
- → are connected interfaces enabled with the same routing protocol?
- → what is the destination subnet and next hop for any static routes?
- → what is the next hop address or interface for any default route?
- → what local routes are advertised with EIGRP **network** command?
- → is default-information originate configured?
- → are connected interfaces assigned to same AS or OSPF area?
- → are connected OSPF interfaces using the same timer intervals?
- → what local routes are advertised with OSPF wildcard mask?
- → what local routes are advertised with RIPv2 **network** command?
- → are subinterfaces assigned to correct VLAN and subnet per host?

Access Control Lists

- → what interfaces have an access list applied?
- → what interface and direction is ACL applied to interface?
- → verify permit/deny for hosts, subnets, ports and/or protocols?

*Example: Subnetting Rule*

Layer 3 network interfaces that are directly connected must be assigned to the same subnet. The purpose of subnetting is to create multiple subnets with the same subnet mask length (i.e /30). The IP host address determines what subnet the interface is assigned.

# CCNA IOS Show Commands

The following is a list of the most common IOS commands associated with questions from the CCNA exam. They are all standard IOS commands used to configure, verify and troubleshoot network connectivity. The IOS commands are based on all topics from the published CCNA exam guidelines.

## Cisco CLI Help Facility

### Mode Level

The List of commands available from each Cisco device mode is available with question mark **?** from each top level mode prompt.

>    rommon > **?**
>    switch > **?**
>    switch# **?**
>    switch(config)# **?**
>    switch(config-if)# **?**

### Command Level

The command level **?** provides a list of all commands for that subgroup such as show commands for instance. In addition the question **?** after any IOS command displays syntax options for that specific command. It is a quick reference for correct configuration syntax and commands not supported with the current IOS version.

>    switch# **show ?**
>    switch(config)# **vtp mode ?**
>    switch(config-if)# **?**
>    switch(config-if)# **show interfaces ?**

### Partial Commands

The partial command level question **?** provides a list of all commands that begin with the letters specified. That helps list commands available that start with the same letters.

>    switch# **c?**

## Global Commands

### show running-config
Display the current running configuration script on any Cisco device.

### show version
Display a variety of device information including the following:

- IOS version
- license feature set
- configuration register setting
- hardware

### show protocols
Verify operational status (up/up), IP address and subnet mask of all network interfaces.

### show ip interface brief
Summarizes the operational status (up/up) and IP address of all switch and router interfaces. The *Status* column is equivalent to *Interface* (Layer 1) for show interfaces command. The *Protocol* column is equivalent to *Line Protocol* (Layer 2) for show interfaces command.

### show interfaces [interface]
Display the operational status (up/up), IP address, configuration settings and errors for a specific switch or router interface.

- operational status
- speed
- duplex
- MTU
- interface errors

### show cdp neighbor detail
Display all directly connected neighbor devices and confirm there is Layer 2 connectivity to each neighbor and the following neighbor details:

- local interface
- neighbor hostname
- neighbor interface
- neighbor IOS version
- neighbor hardware platform

### show cdp
Verify that CDP is enabled, update timer, hold timer and CDP version.

### show lldp
Verify that LLDP is enabled and timer settings.

### show lldp neighbors detail
Display all multi-vendor neighbors directly connected to a Cisco device and confirm there is Layer 2 connectivity to each neighbor.

- local interface
- neighbor hostname
- neighbor interface
- neighbor IOS version
- neighbor hardware platform

### show memory
Display the total, used and available memory on a Cisco device.

### show process cpu
Display the CPU utilization for a Cisco device at five minute intervals.

### show environment
Verify the operational status of fans, temperature and power supplies. In addition list the percentage of power supply utilization and what amount is available.

### do [show command]
Run show commands from any device mode prompt.

## LAN Switching Technologies

### show vlan brief
Display all configured VLANs, verify active status and any switch ports assigned.

### show vlan
Display all configured VLANs, verify active status and any switch ports assigned. There is some additional VLAN information provided as well.

### show interface switchport
Display the operational mode and administrative mode for local switch ports and enable status. In addition there is a variety of trunking configuration and VLAN pruning information.

### show interfaces trunk

Verify the operational status of trunk interfaces and list configuration settings:

- switch port members
- allowed VLANs
- native VLAN
- encapsulation type
- trunk mode

### show interfaces status

Display the Layer 2 *connected / notconnect* status for each switch port and configuration settings.

- connected / not connect
- interface speed
- duplex settings
- VLAN
- Ethernet standard

### show etherchannel summary

Verify all EtherChannel links configured on the local switch including the operational status.

- operational status
- channel group number
- negotiation protocol (PAgP/LACP)
- switch ports assigned

### show interface port-channel [number]

Verify the operational status (up/up), configuration and errors for a port channel interface assigned to an EtherChannel.

- IP address
- speed
- duplex
- MTU
- interface errors
- port members

### show interfaces [interface] transceiver

Display the Layer 1 characteristics of the transceiver connected to a switch port.

### show spanning-tree vlan [number]

Display the spanning tree information for a specific VLAN.

- root bridge
- timers
- STP port types (local interfaces)
- port path cost

### show spanning-tree interface [interface]

Display the spanning tree information for a specific switch interface.

- STP port type
- STP port state
- port path cost
- STP timers

### show spanning-tree

Display the bridge ID for the local switch and root bridge ID for each VLAN including priority and timer settings.

- local bridge ID, priority and timers
- root bridge priority per VLAN
- root bridge MAC address per VLAN
- priority and path cost for local switch ports

### show spanning-tree summary

Display the spanning tree protocol enabled on the local switch.

- spanning tree protocol enabled
- root bridge ID for each VLAN
- STP enhancements (PortFast etc.).
- STP port states per VLAN

### show vtp status

Display various configuration information for the VTP domain where the local switch is a member.

- version number
- configuration revision
- operating mode of local switch
- domain name

*show mac address-table*

Display MAC address, port number and VLAN of each host connected to the local switch.

## Routing Technologies

*ping [ip address] [hostname]*

Confirms Layer 3 network connectivity between a source and destination based on sending and return of ICMP packets.

*traceroute [ip address] [hostname]*

Confirm the routing path for Layer 3 connectivity between a source and destination based on UDP packets.

*show ip route*

Display the routing table for the local router that includes all known subnets, routing protocol, next hop address, metrics and administrative distance. In addition the gateway of last resort (default route) is shown when it is configured.

*show ip arp*

Display the IP address and MAC address bindings in the router ARP table. The MAC address of servers and network devices are learned through ARP requests and added to the local cache.

*show ipv6 interface brief*

Verify the operational status (up/up) and IPv6 address for all router interfaces.

*show ipv6 interface [interface]*

Verify the operational status (up/up), IPv6 addressing, configuration settings and errors for a router interface.

- speed
- duplex
- MTU
- interface errors

*show ip protocols*

Display a variety of settings and configuration for all enabled routing protocols on the router.

### show ip ospf

Display various configuration settings for each OSPF process enabled on the router.

- router ID
- timers
- interfaces per area
- area range (subnet)

### show ip ospf neighbor

Verify all OSPF adjacencies established with directly connected OSPF neighbors.

- neighbor router ID
- IP address
- adjacency state
- assigned DR/BDR

### show ip ospf interface [interface]

Verify the operational status (up/up) of an OSPF enabled interface. In addition Display the OSPF configuration for the interface.

- IP address
- area assigned
- process ID
- router ID
- network type
- timers
- assigned DR/BDR
- adjacent neighbor

### show ip ospf database

Display the OSPF link state database topology that includes Link State Advertisements (LSAs) for all OSPF neighbors advertising from all areas.

- link state advertisements
- advertising router
- process ID
- router ID

### show ipv6 ospf interface [interface]

Verify the operational status (up/up) of an OSPF for IPv6 enabled interface. In addition list the IPv6 addressing and OSPF configuration for the interface.

- IPv6 address
- area assigned
- process ID
- network type
- timers
- assigned DR/BDR

### show ipv6 ospf neighbor detail

Display all OSPFv3 for IPv6 adjacencies established with OSPF neighbors.

- neighbor router ID
- IPv6 addressing
- adjacency state
- assigned DR/BDR

### show ip eigrp neighbors

Display all EIGRP adjacencies established with directly connected EIGRP neighbors.

- neighbor IP address
- local interface
- autonomous system number
- hold time
- SRTT, RTO and queue count

### show ip eigrp interfaces

Display all active EIGRP interfaces associated with an autonomous system.

### show ipv6 eigrp neighbors

Display all EIGRP for IPv6 adjacencies established with directly connected neighbors.

- neighbor IPv6 address
- local interface
- autonomous system
- hold time
- SRTT, RTO and queue count

### show ipv6 eigrp interfaces [interface]

Verify all active EIGRP for IPv6 interfaces associated with an autonomous system (AS).

### show ip eigrp topology

Display all successor and feasible successor routes to a destination in addition to DUAL states.

### show ip rip neighbors

Display all active sessions the local router has established with RIPv2 neighbors that include neighbor IP address and interface.

## WAN Technologies

### show interfaces multilink [interface]

Display the IP address and encapsulation type for the multilink interface.

- operational status (up/up)
- interface errors
- LCP / IPCP negotiation status

### show ppp multilink

Verify the multilink interface status as enabled for the router.

- bundle name
- local and remote hostnames
- member interfaces
- packet errors

### show pppoe session

Display all PPP over Ethernet (PPPoE) sessions enabled for the router.

- local and remote MAC address of peers
- local interface
- dialer number

### show ip bgp neighbors

Display all BGP neighbor peering sessions established and TCP connection information. The neighbor configuration includes the following.

- router ID
- IP address
- neighbor feature capabilities

### show ip bgp summary

Display all BGP routing information for the neighbor connections including prefix (subnet), attribute and prefix (subnet) information.

### show interface tunnel *[number]*

Verify the operational status (up/up) of the tunnel and the assigned IP address. In addition the tunnel source address and local interface is shown along with transport configuration.

## Infrastructure Services

### show ip dhcp conflict

Display all IP address conflicts detected on the IOS DHCP server when allocating IP addresses to DHCP clients.

### show ip dhcp binding

Display the IP address and MAC address of DHCP client, lease expiration and assignment type on the IOS DCHP server.

### show ip dhcp snooping

Verify that DHCP snooping is enabled along with assigned VLANs and interfaces configured for snooping. In addition verify the VLANs are operational for snooping.

### show standby

Display the HSRP configuration on the local router for the router group configured.

- virtual IP address
- virtual MAC address
- timers
- active router
- standby router

### show ip nat translations

Verify the NAT addressing assigned for translating between private and public addressing.

## Infrastructure Security

### show port-security interface *[interface]*

Display the port security configuration for a switch interface.

### show dot1x interface *[interface]* details

Display the switch side settings for port-based authentication of a host.

*show access-lists*

Display all IPv4 access control lists configured on the local router to verify filtering of packets.

*show ipv6 access-lists*

Display all IPv6 access control lists configured on the local router to verify filtering of packets.

## Infrastructure Management

*show ntp status*

Verify the synchronization status to an NTP peer, IP address of NTP peer, local stratum level and clock signaling.

*show users all*

Display all inbound connections to the local device including VTY, console and AUX lines.

*show terminal*

Display terminal settings for the current terminal line and transport protocols allowed for remote management access (SSH, Telnet etc.)

*show flash*

List the files currently on flash memory including available memory.

*erase nvram:*

Delete all the files on NVRAM including the startup configuration.

*show logging*

Verify the logging configuration and where it is enabled/disabled on the network device. In addition list all error messages logged for a specific device

# CCNA IOS Configuration Reference

Login to the network device

    router > **enable**
    router# **configure terminal**
    router(config)#

Configure a hostname

    router(config)# **hostname router-1**

Encrypt passwords in configuration files.

    router-1(config)# **service password-encryption**

Configure an enable password *cisconet* with level 15 privilege.

    router-1(config)# **enable password cisconet**

Configure username admin with highest security level and encrypt password.

    router-1(config)# **username admin privilege 15 password 7**

Configure username cisco with user EXEC level and hidden secret password.

    router-1(config)# **username cisco privilege 1 password 5**

Configure Telnet login, set the password to cisco and a timeout value of 5 minutes for all five default VTY lines.

    router-1(config)# **line vty 0 4**
    router-1(config-line)# **password cisco**
    router-1(config-line)# **login**
    router-1(config-line)# **exec-timeout 5**

Configure console port with password *cisco* for local access security.

    router-1(config)# **line console 0**
    router-1(config-line)# **password cisco**
    router-1(config-line)# **login**

Configure an MOTD login banner for a Cisco device.

    router-1(config)# **banner motd** ^ enter text ^

Configure PST timezone on a Cisco device.

> router-1(config)# **clock timezone PST -8**

Generate RSA keys to enable SSH version 2 on a router. The SSH version (1 2) of host client software is supported by the router when no version is configured.

> router-1(config)# **crypto key generate rsa**
> router-1(config)# **ip ssh version 2**
> router-1(config)# **ip ssh timeout 90 authentication-retries 2**

Configure router to only permit inbound SSH connections on default VTY lines.

> router-1(config)# **line vty 0 4**
> router-1(config)# **transport input ssh**

Configure SNMP community string to read-only access with password *cisco*. In addition configure a string with a read/write access and password *simlabs* for additional access.

> switch(config)# **snmp-server community cisco ro**
> switch(config)# **snmp-server community simlabs rw**

Configure a router that will send system messages to a Syslog server that is assigned IP address 192.168.3.1

> router-1(config)# **logging on**
> router-1(config)# **logging host 192.168.3.1**
> router-1(config)# **end**

Configure an external time server as authoritative time source for a router.

> router-1(config)# **ntp server 172.16.1.1**

Configure the IP address of a DNS server (172.16.1.2) where requests are forwarded for resolving hostnames and IP addresses.

> router-1(config)# **ip name-server 172.16.1.2**

Configure the DNS domain name *cloud.cisconet.com* assigned to a router for responding to unqualified DNS queries.

> router-1(config)# **ip domain-name *cloud.cisconet.com***

Configure a switch access port interface and assign VLAN 10.

    switch-1(config)# **switchport mode access**
    switch-1(config)# **switchport access vlan 10**

Configure a switch trunk interface wth native VLAN 999 and allow VLANs 10-12

    switch-1(config)# **switchport mode trunk**
    switch-1(config)# **switchport trunk native vlan 999**
    switch-1(config)# **switchport trunk allowed vlan 10-12**

Configure EtherChannel on a switch port with PAgP desirable mode and assign to channel group 1.

    switch-1(config)# **switchport mode access**
    switch-1(config)# **switchport access vlan 10**
    switch-1(config)# **duplex auto**
    switch-1(config)# **speed auto**
    switch-1(config)# **channel-group 1 mode desirable**

Configure EtherChannel on a switch port with LACP active mode and assign to channel group 1.

    switch-1(config)# **switchport mode access**
    switch-1(config)# **switchport access vlan 10**
    switch-1(config)# **duplex auto**
    switch-1(config)# **speed auto**
    switch-1(config)# **channel-group 1 mode active**

Configure VTP server mode on a switch with password *ccnalab* and VTP domain name *cisconet*.

    switch-1(config)# **vtp mode server**
    switch-1(config)# **vtp password ccnalab**
    switch-1(config)# **vtp domain cisconet**

Configure PortFast and BPDU guard on a switch port interface.

    switch-1(config)# **switchport mode access**
    switch-1(config)# **switchport access vlan 10**
    switch-1(config)# **spanning-tree portfast**
    switch-1(config)# **spanning-tree bpduguard enable**

Configure an access switch with a default gateway for Telnet access.

    switch(config)# **ip default-gateway 172.16.1.3**

Configure CDP globally on a Cisco network device.

    router-1(config)# **cdp run**

Configure LLDP globally on a Cisco network device.

    router-1(config)# **lldp run**

IPv4 static route to destination 172.16.1.1/24 with next hop 172.16.2.1

    router-1(config)# **ip route 172.16.1.1 255.255.255.0 172.16.2.1**

IPv4 default route with next hop of 172.33.1.2

    router-1(config)# **ip route 0.0.0.0/0 172.33.1.2**

IPv6 static route to destination subnet 2001:DB8:3C4D:1::/64

    router-1(config)# **ipv6 unicast-routing**
    router-1(config)# **ipv6 route 2001:DB8:3C4D:1::/64  2001:DB8:3C4D:2::1**

IPv6 default route with next hop of 2001:DB8:3C4D:2::1

    router-1(config)# **ipv6 unicast-routing**
    router-1(config)# **ipv6 route ::/0  2001:DB8:3C4D:2::1**

IPv4 floating static route to destination subnet 192.168.3.1 with AD = 200

    router-1(config)# **ip route 192.168.3.1 255.255.255.0 192.168.2.2 200**

EIGRP for IPv4 single autonomous system global configuration advertising subnet 192.168.1.0/24 and 172.16.3.0/24 to AS 10. Cisco automatically converts a subnet mask when configured to a wildcard mask with EIGRP.

    router-1(config)# **router eigrp 10**
    router-1(config-router)# **network 192.168.1.0 0.0.0.255**
    router-1(config-router)# **network 172.16.3.0 0.0.0.255**

EIGRP for IPv6 globally enabled on router-1 and interface Gi0/0 enabled with EIGRP in autonomous system 1.

    router-1(config)# **ipv6 unicast-routing**
    router-1(config-router)# **router-id 172.16.1.1**

    router-1(config)# **interface gigabitethernet0/0**
    router-1(config-if)# **ipv6 enable**
    router-1(config-if)# **ipv6 eigrp 1**
    router-1(config-if)# **ipv6 router eigrp 1**

OSPFv2 multi-area global configuration that is advertising subnet 192.168.0.0/24 to area 0 and 172.16.1.0/24 to area 1.

    router-1(config)# **router ospf 1**
    router-1(config-router)# **router-id 172.16.1.255**
    router-1(config-router)# **network 192.168.0.0 0.0.255.255 area 0**
    router-1(config-router)# **network 172.16.1.0 0.0.0.255 area 1**

OSPFv3 is enabled on a router interface and assigned to area 0. There are two global commands that enable OSPFv3 for the router. The OSPFv3 global process is assigned to process ID 1 for this example. The interface is enabled when it is assigned to process ID 1 and area 0.

    router(config)# **ipv6 router ospf 1**
    router(config)# **router-id 192.168.1.1**

    router(config)# **interface gigabitethernet0/0**
    router(config-if)# **no ip address**
    router(config-if)# **ipv6 enable**
    router(config-if)# **ipv6 address 2001:AB3E::/64 eui-64**
    router(config-if)# **ipv6 ospf 1 area 0**

RIPv2 globally enabled on router-1 and advertising 172.33.0.0, 192.168.1.0 and 192.168.3.0 subnets. Advertise a default route to all peering RIPv2 neighbors and turn off automatic summarization to enable classless routing.

    router-1(config)# **router rip**
    router-1(config)# **version 2**
    router-1(config)# **network 172.33.0.0**
    router-1(config)# **network 192.168.1.0**
    router-1(config)# **network 192.168.3.0**
    router-1(config)# **default-information originate**
    router-1(config)# **no auto-summary**

Configure subinterfaces on a router to enable Inter-VLAN routing for VLAN 10, VLAN 11 and VLAN 12.

    router-1(config)# **interface gigabitethernet0/0.10**
    router-1(config-subif)# **encapsulation dot1q 10**
    router-1(config-subif)# **ip address 192.168.10.254 255.255.255.0**

    router-1(config-subif)# **interface gigabitethernet0/0.11**
    router-1(config-subif)# **encapsulation dot1q 11**
    router-1(config-subif)# **ip address 192.168.11.254 255.255.255.0**

    router-1(config-subif)# **interface gigabitethernet0/0.12**
    router-1(config-subif)# **encapsulation dot1q 12**
    router-1(config-subif)# **ip address 192.168.12.254 255.255.255.0**

Configure a Switch Virtual Interface (SVI) on a switch for Telnet connectivity.

    switch(config)# **interface vlan [number]**
    switch(config-if)# **ip address [ip address] [subnet mask]**
    switch(config-if)# **no shutdown**

Configure port security on a switch interface and add MAC address of the connected host to the running configuration. In addition, limit the number of hosts for the switch port to a maximum of one.

    switch(config-if)# **switchport port-security**
    switch(config-if)# **switchport port-security mac-address sticky**
    switch(config-if)# **switchport port-security maximum 1**

Configure HSRP on an interface with router-1 as active for group 1 and enable HSRPv2 protocol features. In addition enable virtual IP address of 172.16.3.1 for the HSRP group 1.

    router-1(config)# **interface gigabitethernet0/1**
    router-1(config-if)# **ip address 172.16.1.1 255.255.255.0**
    router-1(config-if)# **standby version 2** (*enables HSRPv2*)
    router-1(config-if)# **standby 1 preempt** (*compare priorities for group 1*)
    router-1(config-if)# **standby 1 priority 110** (*active router*)
    router-1(config-if)# **standby 1 ip 172.16.1.3** (*virtual IP address*)

Configure NAT on a router with a pool of public addresses named *inet* and *overload* keyword for Port Address Translation. In addition configure an ACL to enable hosts from subnet range 192.168.1.0/24 to use internet.

    R1(config)# **ip nat pool inet 172.33.1.1 172.33.1.9 netmask 255.255.255.0**
    R1(config)# **ip nat inside source list 100 pool inet overload**
    R1(config)# **access-list 100 permit ip 192.168.1.0 0.0.0.255 any**

Configure external BGP on a local router for peering with a remote BGP peer. Assign local router to private AS 65535 and neighbor to 65534 with assigned 172.16.1.2 address. Advertise subnet 10.10.34.1/24 to the remote peer.

    router-1(config)# **router bgp 65535**
    router-1(config-router)# **neighbor 172.16.1.2 remote-as 65534**
    router-1(config-router)# **network 10.10.34.1 mask 255.255.255.0**

# CCNA Test Strategies

The following are recommended best practices when taking the CCNA certification exam. Manage your time effectively and optimize your exam readiness.

- ✓ Subnetting is a key aspect of the CCNA exam for both theoretical and lab simulation questions. It is easy as well to make mistakes when converting between binary and decimal values. Write all class B and class C subnets on paper when the exam starts. Include the number of hosts available per subnet and conversion charts.

- ✓ Don't burn time with a question you could only guess on. Take your best guess eliminating options you know are not correct and move on to the next question.

- ✓ Take some practice tests that are 90 minutes long to verify you are scoring at least 80% and have honed your time management skills properly. It is helpful to practice complex questions with show commands and drawings.

- ✓ Do not waste time considering your answers from previous questions.

- ✓ Take your time with SIM questions. Verify the answers carefully noting any syntax or configuration errors missed or not included before submitting. Do not click next until you have answered each question.

- ✓ Complex questions are sometimes comprised of convoluted wording, drawings and show command listings. Consider fundamentally what the question is testing.

- ✓ Make notes when going through books and labs to summarize key points, rules and commands for exam day review. For example IPv6 addressing rules or ACL configuration to permit or deny protocols from a single subnet.

- ✓ Read each question a couple of times carefully (to make a well-worn point). Note the subtleties with each question that Cisco employs and what the question is really asking.

The following is an example of wording for a typical CCNA style question.

What command will verify that an interface is operational and responding?

    A. show interfaces
    B. show ip interface brief
    C. telnet
    **D. ping**

The key word <u>responding</u> is used here and that implies sending a packet to an interface and verifying the packet returns.

- The commands *show interfaces* and *show ip interface brief* are wrong. You are at the device and there is no connectivity so no send/return of packets occurs.

- Telnet is wrong. Telnet is an application layer protocol and confirms all layers are working correctly. The device could be operational and have an incorrect Telnet configuration. The interface is operational at Layer 2 and responds to ping at Layer 3.

Ping is best answer. ICMP packet is sent to the interface and return message is destination unreachable or packet received to confirm the interface is operational.

Made in the USA
San Bernardino, CA
07 August 2019